To my friend
Dr. Reuben W. Hahn
pioneer
in the church's campus ministry

# Acknowledgments

I hope you will find some adaptable stuff in these pages. Make it your own. Add to it from your personal pastoral experience. And then pass it on.

I applaud Jessica Wilmarth (†) for her usual outstanding work at the computer; Wayne Morton for many helpful suggestions; and Mervin A. Marquardt, David Koch, and Wilbert Rosin for their editorial expertise.

In what follows I give credit first of all for some of the content in two sermons: "The Keys of the Kingdom" and "Are You a Tame Captive of Your Community?" The thanks go to Robert K. Menzel, who died in 1989. In the 1950s we frequently shared materials and wrote sermons in concert. I also credit P.H.D. Lang, Edward W. Wessling, and Richard Lischer for helpful source material. I thank Mervin A. Marquardt for the Memorial Day outline.

Some sermons are adapted from material by the author in *The Concordia Pulpit* (St. Louis: Concordia Publishing House): "Are You a Doubting Thomas?" adapted from *Concordia Pulpit, 1984,* 134–38. "The Art of Competing with Yourself," adapted from *Concordia Pulpit, 1973,* 220-25. "Capturing a Spirit of Thankfulness" is adapted from Donald L. Deffner, *Bound to Be Free: The Quest for Inner Freedom* (Fort Wayne, Indiana: Concordia Theological Seminary Press, © Donald L. Deffner), 71-77.

Some illustrations are from Richard Andersen and Donald L. Deffner, *For Example: Illustrations for Contemporary Preaching* (St. Louis: Concordia Publishing House, 1977).

Some illustrations are from Donald L. Deffner, *Seasonal Illustrations for Preaching and Teaching* (San Jose: Resource Publications, Inc. 160 E. Virginia Street #290, San Jose, California 95112–5876). Special thanks go to Resource Publications, Inc., for permission to quote.

Some illustrations are from Donald L. Deffner, *At Life's End,* (St. Louis: Concordia, 1995); *At the Death of a Child: Words of Comfort and Hope* (St. Louis: Concordia, 1993); *The Best of Your Life Is the Rest of Your Life* (Nashville: Abingdon, 1977); *Bold Ones on Campus: A Call for Christian Commitment* (St. Louis: Concordia, 1973); *The Bright Red Sports Car and Other Stories* (St. Louis: Concordia, 1993); *The Possible Years: Thoughts After Thirty on Christian Adulthood* (St. Louis: Concordia, 1973); *Prayers for People Under Pressure* (Milwaukee: Northwestern Publishing House, 1992); *The Unlocked Door and Other Stories* (St. Louis: Concordia, 1994; see also *The Secret Admirer and Other Stories* [St. Louis: Concordia, 1994]); *Windows into the Lectionary: Seasonal Illustrations for Preaching and Teaching* (San Jose, California: Resource Publications, Inc., 1996); *You Say You're Depressed? How God Helps You Overcome Anxieties* (Nashville: Abingdon, 1976).

Some illustrations are from Walter B. Knight, *Three Thousand Illustrations for Christian Service* (Grand Rapids: Wm. B. Eerdmans Publishing Company, 1947).

# Contents

# Scriptural Index

**Genesis 2:18**
  Wedding I

**Deuteronomy 6:5–9, 20–25**
  Father's Day

**Proverbs 31:28–31**
  Mother's Day

**Isaiah 61:10**
  Wedding III

**Matthew 16:18–19**
  Ordination/Installation of a Pastor

**Mark 12:30**
  Stewardship

**John 20:19–31**
  St. Thomas, Apostle—December 21

**Romans 2:14–15 and Titus 3:1–8**
  Memorial Day

**Romans 12:2**
  Dedication/Anniversary of a Church

**1 Corinthians 12:1–11**
  Labor Day

**1 Corinthians 15:55**
  Funeral II

**Galatians 2:20**
  The Conversion of St. Paul, Apostle—January 25

**Colossians 3:3, 13**
Wedding II

**1 Thessalonians 4:17**
Funeral I

**1 Thessalonians 4:13a, 17b**
Funeral III

**1 Thessalonians 5:18**
Day of Special or National Thanksgiving

**Titus 3:1–8 and Romans 2:14–15**
Memorial Day

# Preface

## "Topical" Sermons

Some preachers may designate the messages which follow as "topical" sermons. I affirm that fact and in the same breath challenge the pejorative note often implied in the term "topical." Indeed, I would like to redeem "topical" preaching, if by that we mean "sermons with a single, clear idea."

The great preacher John Henry Jowett once stated:

> No sermon is ready for preaching, nor ready for writing out, until we can express its theme in a short, pregnant sentence as clear as crystal. I find the getting of that sentence the hardest, the most exacting, and the most fruitful labor in my study. To compel oneself to fashion that sentence, to dismiss every word that is vague, ragged, ambiguous, to think oneself through to a form of words that defines the theme with scrupulous exactness—this is surely one of the most vital and essential factors in the making of a sermon; and I do not think any sermon ought to be preached or even written, until that sentence has emerged, clear and lucid as a cloudless moon. (*The Preacher, His Life and Work* [New York: Doran, 1912], 133)

The error in not developing that "one clear idea" is that the preacher may try to "cover" (rather than uncover!) every verse in the text, assuming that such an approach is "expositional preaching." Or, the sermonizer may wander over all three lessons for the day, trying to do "liturgical justice" to them, rather than correlating the propers, but sticking to one central homiletical concept.

Henry Mitchell also affirms the "main idea" principle in sermon organization. "If real communication rather than a show of erudition is the goal, one good idea will be a quite satisfying achievement." (*The Recovery of Preaching* [New York: Harper and Row, 1977], 43.)

And Fred Craddock notes that the ability to capture the meaning of the text in one sentence "marks a genuine achievement, rewarded not only by a sense of satisfaction but by a new appetite for the next task: the sermon itself." (*Preaching* [Nashville: Abingdon Press, 1985], 122.)

To those who disdain topical preaching, I contended in *Compassionate Preaching: A Primer/Primer in Homiletics* (Fort Wayne: Concordia Seminary Press, 1991, 78) that there is such a thing as bad exegetical/expositional preaching. Some of the marks of that are

- Too much exegesis dragged into the pulpit
- Dull verse-by-verse commentary on text
- Presumption that the sheer statement of Bible truth equals communication
- People often are left to make their own application
- A rambling over several textual ideas, failing to focus on one central theme.

I pointed out that there also is such a thing as bad topical preaching. Its marks include

- Alluding to the text without developing it
- Weak on biblical content
- Long on "religious"/moral talk.

In between these two extremes I put *good* exegetical/expositional preaching and *good* topical preaching—which are one and the same! This type of sermon is biblical and fully textual, yet it addresses one clear theme instead of wandering around. The exegesis is implicit, and the interpretation of the text is thorough. Plus, both are applied to life in the light of that "one, clear idea."

Richard R. Caemmerer said that the preacher can get 19 different sermons on one text. "But you will be preaching on this text again. Today focus on one aspect of the text."

That is what I have sought to do. And I have attempted to provide a fresh tack or different direction in preaching at specific occasions, also using free texts. Though sometimes "topical," my first and foremost objective still has been biblical/textual preaching. And it has focused on the "one, clear idea" succinctly stated in a Law/Gospel, problem/resolution theme.

# Are You a Doubting Thomas?

## John 20:19-31

The pastor's family had just gotten home from church and was anticipating the Sunday feast. Still in their Sunday best they awaited the signal from Mom. The first sign that the meal was almost ready was the command, "Boys, be sure and wash your hands. We don't want any germs at the table. Be sure and use soap and hot water. That will get rid of any germs that you might have caught."

That was not quite what the boys wanted to hear. Washing was such an inconvenience. And all this talk about germs— what were they anyway? Was this germs talk all a trick to get them to wash their hands so that Mom's white table cloth would stay clean?

The seven-year-old reluctantly made his way toward the washroom mumbling to himself, "Jesus and germs, Jesus and germs! That's all I hear, and I never see either one of them."

In your life today can you relate to that little boy? Is your faith one in which you need to see in order to believe, or do you believe without seeing? In the Gospel lesson for today Jesus shows us that he desires us to have faith in him—to believe—without seeing. (Paul Arndt in *Seasonal Illustrations,* 84-85)

And that is my theme: <u>Although we are inclined to doubt God at times, he calls us to a larger faith, a greater faith, a stronger faith.</u>

Doubt was the problem of Thomas. He had been with the Lord for a long time. Thomas believed in him, but his faith wavered when the other disciples told him, "We have seen the Lord"—the resurrected Christ. He wanted some proof that Jesus was not still lying in the tomb. "Unless I see the nail marks in his hands and put my finger where the nails were, and put my hand into his side, I will not believe it," he said

13

(v. 25). Quite a laundry list for requirements for faith, isn't it!

But note what happens eight days later. Our Lord appears to the disciples, Thomas being present now. His first words are words of calm, peace, and comfort—not fear. "Peace be with you," he says. And then he challenges Thomas to the pragmatic test of actually putting his fingers into the wounds he suffered on the cross for us. He confronts Thomas with "Stop doubting and believe!"

And do you know what happened? Some people may imagine Thomas approaching Christ gingerly, touching a wound here and there, then standing back and making a judgment. "Well, Lord, I guess it really is you after all." But that's not what happened. Thomas simply confessed his faith—immediately, "My Lord and my God!"

The compassionate Christ responded with words which apply both to Thomas and to you and me here today. Jesus said, "Because you have seen me, you have believed; blessed are those who have not seen and yet have believed."

## The "Unless" Christian

Listen to that challenge coming down from 2,000 years ago to you and me worshiping the risen Christ in this place right now: "Blessed are those who have not seen and yet have believed" (v. 29).

Thomas said, "Unless I see … I will not believe."

Do you feel like I sometimes do? "Lord, I am so lonely. Unless you make somebody 'reach out and touch someone'— namely, me!—I am going to think no one, especially you, cares for me anymore."

Are you like me when I often feel, "Lord, unless you show me the answer to my financial problems, my problems at school, the illness which confronts me, the future which threatens me—unless you come across, I'm really not going to believe in you as my loving, helping Father anymore."

Are you like me when I am tempted to doubt God's desire to be a personal, daily reality in my life? "*Unless … unless …*

14

*unless* … I will not believe in you."

But you and I can't make deals with God. Our relationship with him is to be unconditional. He says to us, "Believe in me, and I will show you more than you ever dreamed could happen in your life."

This is not a "think positive and you will get ahead in your business or marriage" kind of thinking. Rather, this is Jesus asking us to notice the people in his ministry who saw the release of Christ's power: the Roman centurion, the demon-afflicted man, the woman with the hemorrhage, the paralyzed man, and many more. He said, "Your sins are forgiven. Pick up your bed and go home. *Your faith has saved you!"*

So I challenge you in your own personal life. God is a God who doesn't make deals. He will escape you forever, until you see him revealed in Jesus his Son. Why in the world do you insist on knocking yourself out, pounding on his almighty front door when it has already been opened through the gift of faith in his Son? That faith brings us into a relationship with him that lasts forever.

A Christian was talking about the age-old problem of human suffering. "Why does God allow it?" he asked. A friend of his answered, "This much I know. I have seen a lieutenant send one of his men, a dear and trusted friend, to certain death because the mission had to be accomplished. The private spent no time in asking why; he saluted and went. In my own life sometimes I do not know why—but I am not asking. I am just saluting, if that is my post." (Source unknown)

In your own life, are you willing, no matter what confronts you, to say, "God knows. He has a reason for permitting this to happen. I trust him. That's enough for me"?

## The Difficulty of Faith

That is Jesus' challenge and loving call to you and me—as it was to Thomas. "Stop doubting and believe." But it's not easy, is it? For the life of faith produces conflicts for us. To "walk by faith and not by sight" in this day and age is to live a life which confronts real difficulties in our hearts and in the world all around us. Everything we see and read and hear is constantly attacking the "walk of faith."

It's not a new problem. Throughout the New Testament there are repeated failures as far as the matter of faith is concerned. The apostle Paul wrote sadly about one of his temporary co-workers, "Demas, because he loved this world, has deserted me" (2 Tim. 4:10). Demas wasn't the first or last who found the "faith life" too hard to take, too demanding when compared to his own desires and needs.

But that's the challenge of Jesus to Thomas and to you and me. Under the most trying of circumstances he asks, "Do you have faith in me?"

A minister tells of a happy and efficient wife of a fellow pastor, a woman who was experiencing her full share of life's sunshine and shade, but with no real darkness falling her way. And then, suddenly, without warning, her husband died of a heart attack, leaving her terribly alone and afraid; afraid of her own decisions, afraid of the present, afraid of the future.

Following a visit with his colleague's widow, he related that she was in the vice-like grip of fear—so tyrannized that most of her time was spent in bed. She was so terrified that she became bedridden.

When the minister saw her two years later, he was pleasantly surprised to find a poised, serene woman, working as a receptionist in an insurance office. When the pastor asked her to explain her amazing recovery, the woman replied, "Work helped, of course; but I couldn't work at all until I faced my fear and saw it was basically a selfish rebellion against God and what I thought was God's will. When I saw that, I began to pray that God would forgive my selfishness. As I prayed, I became aware of God's hand reaching down to me, and the Holy Spirit moved me to reach up in faith until I finally clasped that hand. And then to my amazement, I found his hand clasping mine; and I knew that he really cared and that he would help me as long as I held his hand in faith." (*Lent, A Time for Renewal,* 106–7)

Some Christians, although they know the true God, are prone to waver and fall when the first winds of adversity strike them. We need to look again and again at the faith of the great reformer Martin Luther. There was a man with a large faith, a strong faith, a great faith in a great God. Certainly he had his doubts and difficulties. Often he faltered when he came to the point of Scripture that says that God is good and that he is good to me. But then he would realize the meaning of "the righteousness of God" and that this righteousness is transferred to us when we confess our sin and trust solely in the merits of Christ's death and resurrection—for us.

Yes, Christ's death and resurrection atones for our sins of doubt and weakness of faith. Luther believed that. Do you?

Luther was wise enough to take God at his Word and to trust the Holy Spirit to give him the power of faith. He knew it was God who saved him. That is why Luther was a giant of faith. In the face of all his foes, he cried out, "Here I stand ... I cannot recant ... I can do no other!"

His greatest aid in his struggle was the Holy Scriptures. "The true Christian pilgrimage is not to Rome ... but to the prophets, the psalms, and the Gospels," he said. That was his ground for certainty, the source of faith in Christ. There in the inspired Holy Scriptures he found "a firm foundation."

Feelings come and feelings go,
and feelings are deceiving.
My warrant is the Word of God.
Naught else is worth believing.
(attributed to Luther)

Your strength for this difficult life by faith is in the unfailing witness to Christ, the Holy Scriptures. "For you are all the children of God by faith in Christ Jesus." In Scripture you meet Jesus face to face.

You meet him also in the visible Word, the Blessed Sacrament of the Altar, when Christ comes to us in his body and blood. His presence answers our prayer near the end of one of our services: "We implore you that of your mercy you would strengthen us through the same in faith toward you and in fervent love toward one another."

It's easy to become a doubting Thomas. The life of faith is very difficult. So many pressures around us, tempting us not to live it! We are also lazy and self-centered. But Christ says to you and me again today, "Are you—as I challenged Thomas—willing to 'walk by faith and not by sight'? Blessed are those who have not seen and yet have believed."

## Blessed Are You

By the power of the Holy Spirit, I assure you again today that this faith is a gift from God to you that is yours as you repent of your sins and trust in the healing power of Christ. Your Baptism has saved you from sin and death and made you a child of God. And now, as you remain one of the children of God, Christ continues to forgive and work in you through faith, breaking through your doubts, your self-sufficiency, and your despair. And he says to you as he did to doubting Thomas, "Blessed are you. You haven't found all the answers to the questions in your life, but you still have believed in me. Blessed are you."

There was a woman in a community who was well known for her simple faith and great calm in the midst of many trials. Another woman who had never met her but had heard of her came to visit one day. "I must find out the secret of her calm, happy life," she thought to herself.

As she met her she said, "So you are the woman with the great faith I've heard so much about."

"No," came the reply. "I am not the woman with the great faith, but I am the woman with the little faith in the great God." (*Three Thousand Illustrations,* 258)

Can you say the same? What will it be for you today—an artificial God to whom you pray, "Unless you come through this time, I'm not going to go along with you," or, by the power of the Holy Spirit, a "little" more faith in the great God revealed in Jesus Christ who challenged Thomas and who confronts you again here today?

God turns our lives around. You may not have all the solutions to the problems that confront you, but you know that he is with you every step of the way. He was willing to come down from on high and become one of us in his Son, Jesus Christ, so that we might see what he is really like and learn to know him!

What a great God we have!

### ◆ Closing Prayer ◆

Almighty and ever-living God, as you through the Word of your beloved Son mightily strengthened the faith of the apostle Saint Thomas, keep also us steadfast in the faith by that same Word through all our days; through Jesus Christ, our Lord, who lives and reigns with you and the Holy Spirit, one God, now and forever. Amen.

# Cut Down the Whole Tree!

### Galatians 2:20

[Chapel address, Concordia Theological Seminary, Fort Wayne, Indiana, January 25, 1989, by the author. Adapted from *Bound to Be Free,* 132–33.]

One of the most dramatic and world-renowned shifts from "I" to God is the conversion of C. S. Lewis. This little man, who held the Chair of Medieval and Renaissance Literature at Cambridge, sat in his study without typewriter or secretary and penned the great masterpieces that made him perhaps the most broadly read Christian writer of our century. C. S. Lewis was an agnostic but was *Surprised by Joy* (the title of a book in which he tells about "The Shape of My Early Life" as Christ replaced the "I" in his life).

Lewis describes the exchange between self-will and God's will in *Beyond Personality* (New York: The Macmillan Company, 1947, 40), and his words are a challenge to you and to me:

> Christ says, "Give me all. I don't want so much of your money and so much of your work—I want you. I have not come to torment your natural self, but to kill it. No half-measures are any good. I don't want to cut off a branch here and there, I want to have the whole tree down. I don't want to drill the tooth, or crown it, stop it, but to have it out. Hand over the whole natural self. … I will give you a new self instead. In fact I will give you myself, my own will shall become yours."

Today we celebrate the conversion of St. Paul, Apostle. The commemoration of this event is significant because it marks the beginning of the Apostle Paul's ministry—which affected the whole Christian church.

For the Apostle Paul this matter of handing over one's whole self to Christ to be annihilated was at the heart of Christianity. He wrote the Roman Christians, "For we know that our old self was crucified with him [Christ] so that the body of sin might be done away with, that we should no longer be slaves to sin" (Rom. 6:6). And as he wrote the Colossians, "You died, and your life is now hidden with Christ in God" (Col. 3:3).

How can these words be true for us, when we, not Christ, are so often still at the center of our lives?

The solution is, we are forgiven people. God himself gives us the desire and the ability to give ourselves to be molded by his hands. As converted agnostic Chad Walsh put it, "Here is the mystery and the paradox. The person who uses his freedom to give his 'I' into the hands of God, there to be remade in the image of Christ, is really only lending it. For God gives it back. One day, when you least expect it, he returns it to you, much improved from the scrubbing and alterations it has received." (*Campus Gods on Trial,* [New York: Macmillan, 1962], 87) We may think we are surrendering to a master, but he is raising us as sons and daughters.

St. Augustine was a famous church father who lived in the fourth century. During his youth his life was marked by sexual excesses and profligacy. But his conversion made a dramatic change in his life, and he had a profound influence on African Christianity.

It is said that during his later years he was walking through an area he had earlier haunted as a dissolute youth. A prostitute saw him from her window and shouted down, "Augustine! It is I!" But he continued walking.

Again the woman called out after him, "Augustine! Augustine! It is I!"

But Augustine, without turning his face, walked determinedly ahead, saying, "But it is not I!" He, like St. Paul, had been transformed. (Source unknown)

Today we thank the Lord of all the universes for the gift to us of St. Paul, Apostle. May his confession be ours: "I no longer live, but Christ lives in me. The life I live in the body, I live by faith in the Son of God, who loved me and gave himself for me" (Gal. 2:20).

### ◆ Closing Prayer ◆

Almighty God, as you turned the heart of him who perse-cuted the church and by his preaching caused the light of the Gospel to shine throughout the world, grant us ever to rejoice in the saving light of your Gospel and to spread it to the utter-most parts of the earth; through Jesus Christ, your son, our Lord, who lives and reigns with you and the Holy Spirit, one God, now and forever. Amen.

# Capturing a Spirit of Thankfulness

### 1 Thessalonians 5:18

It is the fall of 1789. You are standing in the presence of President George Washington. He speaks.

> Whereas it is the duty of all nations to acknowledge the providence of Almighty God, to obey his will, to be grateful for his benefits, and humbly implore his protection, aid and favors …
>
> Now, therefore, I do recommend and assign Thursday, the 26th day of November next, to be devoted by the people of these States to the service of that great and glorious Being, who is the Beneficent Author of all the good that was, that is, or that will be; that we may then all unite in rendering unto him our sincere and humble thanks for his kind care and protection of the people of this country, and for all the great and various favors which he has been pleased to confer upon us. (*Three Thousand Illustrations*, 687–88)

That was the first time a president of the United States of America proclaimed a national Thanksgiving Day. But for Christians, every day is Thanksgiving Day. As our text says, "Be thankful in all circumstances. This is what God wants of you in your life in union with Christ Jesus." Or as J. B. Phillips paraphrases it, "Be thankful, whatever the circumstances may be."

And that leads to my question to you this morning: Are you praising God in the midst of everything, no matter how it is going for you? Have you learned to be thankful to God while in the most difficult of times?

That's my theme today: <u>Although we are inclined at times to be discontent or only occasionally thankful to God, he calls us to a thankful spirit and to praise him in all circumstances.</u>

Listen to that Scripture again. Phillips paraphrases: "Be thankful, whatever the circumstances may be." "In everything give thanks," the NKJV puts it. And "everything" means that God is in everything, in bad things as well as good. Now, this does not make God the author of evil; rather, it says that we can see his hand working in all things. Whether it's the instance of the incredible sufferings he permitted Job to go through or the trials he permitted Joseph to experience in being sold into slavery in Egypt, "God meant it for good" (Gen. 50:20 NKJV).

The Christian's clue, then, to capturing the spirit of thankfulness and praise is to be ready at all times—no matter what the difficulties may be—to ask the question, "Lord, what is your will for me in this situation?" Do you always ask that question when problems beset you? You know, if we don't accept the circumstances God's permissive will has allowed, he may permit the difficulties to heap up. For most of us, that might be the only way he can get our attention.

**God Means It Unto Good**

A pastor friend of mine says he always has two lists of the people in his congregation. One is the list of the people who are sick, and he's praying they'll get well. The other lists people who are well, and he's praying they'll get sick! Or, as one writer put it, "The knees of some people are so stiff that sometimes God has to knock their owners down before they'll make use of them" in prayer.

Yet at the same time, when our trials and troubles pile up, the Lord means it unto good. For in our despair he offers us his help. "Cast all your anxiety on him because he cares for you" (1 Peter 5:7). Can you do that? We're going to have to realize our dependence on him before the process will work. As Brother Lawrence said in his classic *Practice of the Presence of God,* "Lord, I cannot do this unless thou enablest me ... It is thou who must hinder my falling, and mend what is amiss." Now *there*, Catherine Marshall said, is a "prayer of helplessness" that can become the "power of helplessness!" (Both Brother Lawrence's and Catherine Marshall's words are in *Beyond Our Selves* [Carmel, New York: Guideposts Associates, Inc., 1961], 148–49)

As God said to St. Paul about his problem, "My grace is all you need, for my power is greatest when you are weak." Paul went on to comment, "I am most happy, then, to be proud of my weaknesses, in order to feel the protection of Christ's power over me. I am content with weaknesses, insults, hardships, persecutions, and difficulties for Christ's sake. For when I am weak, then I am strong" (2 Cor. 12:9–10 TEV). In your personal Christian life, can you say that along with the Apostle Paul, "When I am weak, then I am strong"?

No one likes to be down in the pits, but that's where the action is, and that's where we meet face to face the one who went into the very pits of hell for us.

"If God is for us, who can be against us? He who did not spare his own Son, but gave him up for us all—how will he not also, along with him, graciously give us all things?" (Rom. 8:31–32). As Luther put it, "There is a certain utter despair of one's own ability which must come about before one is prepared to receive the grace of Christ."

So, when you and I are at the very bottom, often only then do we really see God's purpose (and he may delay that insight for some time to come). Often only when we are completely empty of ourselves do we see God at work. God has no use for cups half-full. He wants us completely empty so he can fill us up with himself. That's why you and I need to learn to say with Paul, "I have learned in whatever state I am, to be content" and to "rejoice in the Lord always. Again I will say, rejoice! ... In everything by prayer and supplication, with thanksgiving, let your requests be made known to God" (Phil. 4:11, 4, 6 NKJV).

## No Moralism

Now, this is not an oughta-gotta-needa-shoulda sermon: "You ought to do this or that to be a Christian; you gotta have a spirit of thankfulness if you want to be a 'real' Christian." A true preacher of God does not preach about good works and then say "do this." Good works are *God's* results of preaching. *My* task is to preach the Gospel. Good works—in this instance, evidencing a spirit of thankfulness—spontaneously flow from a Spirit-empowered faith. We by ourselves are unable to do the good; we fail utterly. But the Gospel works through us because of Christ's death on the cross for our sins. He is now at work in us and does that in us which we are unable to do.

Our "spirit of thankfulness" is not a technique we master on our own. Rather, throwing ourselves wholly on God's mercy, Christ takes over in our lives. Only then do others see the change. As Scripture says, "Let your light so shine before men, that they may see your good works and glorify your Father in heaven" (Matt. 5:16 NKJV).

In the examples I am going to cite, note that the individuals gave *God* the glory, for he put the spirit of thankfulness into their hearts. They didn't muster it up on their own.

Take the instance of a young woman of 20, who, after a horrible accident, was so crippled that she could only type with pencils tied to her hands. Writing to her campus pastor and thanking him for the 2,000 cards she had received from fellow students, she stated:

> My condition isn't so bad. I can move my arms slightly, shrug my shoulders, turn my neck, and raise my wrists. I guess that doesn't sound like much, but in all honesty I like it this way. My whole personality changed with my accident, and I became a better person. I used to lie in bed and say "Please, God, let me walk." Over and over I said, "Please, God." And something or someone changed it in my mind, and I found myself saying, "Suzie, why don't you 'please God'? It was so strange how it happened! I truly think that it was a miracle. Many things like that happened to me—and still do. It is an education in itself. Sometimes I think (I should say "know") that people miss a lot out of life by not taking the time to realize that the whole concept of life is giving to others, no matter how much [or little] one has to give. My philosophy on life sure has changed. (From an account by Edward W. Wessling)

Truly, "We know that in all things God works for good with those who love him" (Rom. 8:28 TEV).

Or hear the words of a young mother who barely escaped

death with her two boys and her husband in an auto accident. He was completely encased in the car from his neck down, with just a few inches of clearance all around his head. A truck doing 75 mph hit them head on, killing the driver. She wrote,

> So we are all back together for Christmas and are very thankful. The Scripture, Ephesians 5:20, "Giving thanks always for all things unto God and the Father in the name of our Lord Jesus Christ" [KJV] really had an impact on me the night of the accident after we got to a hospital. During one of my husband's brief conscious moments I told him that the boys and I were fine—and he immediately responded by thanking and praising God. It really spoke to my heart to see him lying there in all his pain and still able to thank God for the situation. Nearly all his cuts have healed completely now, and he will have only very minor scars on his face. His ear seems to be healing, so he'll keep his hearing, and the surgery that put a pin in his left leg just below his hip is doing fine. He is up and about on crutches now and doesn't even look as if he was in a wreck. This whole experience has really shown us how true Philippians 4:19 is: "But my God shall supply all your need according to his riches in glory by Christ Jesus" [KJV]. The Lord really has provided our every need in everything, even down to the tiny details. I wish I could somehow express the joy and peace we feel for having gone through this experience and all it has taught us. (From a Christmas letter to the author)

Or, consider what happened to Doris Beetz, who owned and managed the West Coast Church Supply Store in South San Francisco, California. Here also is an outstanding example of Christian praise and thankfulness to God. In one year, in spite of business difficulties, working 12–16 hours a day, being beaten in a robbery (and in the hospital several weeks), being robbed again, and then having a car crash through the plate glass window of the store, Doris wrote her customers, "God watched over us during the long commutes; God blessed us with good health and helped us keep our enthusiasm … for the ministry we perform in the store." Truly an example of praising God in all things! (From a Christmas letter to the author)

In all these instances, the people were free of morbid introspection, free of self-pity, free to thank God for their circumstance.

## God's Promises

Have you, by the Spirit's power, captured the spirit of thankfulness even in the most trying circumstances? Do you, by the power of the Holy Spirit, see God's loving hand behind it all? "For I know the thoughts that I think toward you, saith the Lord, thoughts of peace, and not of evil" (Jer. 29:11 KJV). With God giving you the grace, you can ask, "Lord, what is your will for me in the midst of these circumstances?"

Having so prayed, look back in time and, with the Spirit's perspective, find God's blessings which you may have over-looked—and thank him for the cumulative effect of his good-ness and love in your life. From the day of your Baptism you have been his child and heir. With that affirmation, then look ahead and be prepared to be thankful in whatever circum-stance is going to come.

This is not just a matter of gritting your teeth to get through adversity. Rather, God's "dare" to you comes with his promise of strength and care.

> No temptation has overtaken you that is not common to man. God is faithful, and he will not let you be tempted beyond your strength, but with the temptation will also provide the way of escape, that you may be able to endure it (1 Cor. 10:13 RSV).

> As your days, so shall your strength be (Deut. 33:25 RSV).

> Underneath are the everlasting arms (Deut. 33:27 RSV).

> "Fear not, for I am with you, be not dismayed, for I am your God; I will strengthen you, I will help you, I will uphold you with my vic-torious right hand" (Is. 41:10 RSV).

The promises are clear. The problem is, you and I often don't really believe them. So, right here and now, repent for the times you failed to trust and thank and praise him. Cast your cares upon him, for he really cares about you—so much that he sent his Son to suffer and die for you.

And now, may the Holy Spirit, first given to you in your Baptism, increase your faith and prepare you for the changes in your life which will surely come, but which you need not fear to see. In the little things of your life today, prepare for the big emergencies tomorrow. On the ordinary road you travel right now, get ready for the mountain tomorrow. In the green pastures and by the still waters prepare yourself for the valley of the shadow.

For when you immerse yourself in the "Means of Grace"— God's Holy Word and the Sacraments—when you live in the Lord, then when you reach the mountain, the shadow, the emergency, you will be God-possessed. He will dwell in you, and you in him.

Put your trust in the Lord, and you will know how to live in the present. Live by God's grace and forgiveness in the present, and the future will not frighten you.

Is your place a small place?
Tend it with care!—He set you there.
Is your place a large place?
Guard it with care!—He set you there.
Whate'er your place, it is
Not yours alone, but his
Who set you there.
(John Oxenham, 1861–1941)

# The True Crowns of Marriage

### Genesis 2:18

[I credit Edward W. Wessling for some of the seed thoughts in this message.]

In the wedding ceremony in the Greek Orthodox Church, crowns are placed over the heads of the couple being married. They "rule for the day." And the whole worshiping community honors them and prays for their joyous life in the Lord.

NAME and NAME, we accept your reign this day. We pray "thy kingdom come," and in a special sense it really does come in this hour, for God gives us the flavor of the kingdom of heaven in his Word.

It is a kingdom of celebration, a kingdom of joy, a kingdom of his love flowing into your love for each other, a love that is beyond reason and longer than life, and stronger than death. In this kingdom, the real crowns you wear are the crowns of eternal life which Christ has promised you through your Baptism, which you are in now, and which will adorn your life throughout your marriage, that others may know you are Christians and be drawn to him who is the source of your eternal life: God himself.

It is from him in Scripture that we learn the true purpose of marriage. First of all, he says it is for the purpose of mutual companionship and the fulfillment of that wonderful desire to love, which he has placed inside of us. "It is not good for the man [or the woman] to be alone," God said (Gen. 2:18). And so marriage offers that completion which only the other person can supply: emotionally, physically, mentally, spiritually.

And from this flows the second purpose of marriage: new lives and new life. This union between man and woman is so deep and complete that from it come new lives, a new existence for each of you—and there can be new life: God's gift of children.

## The Twin Nature of the Vows

These, then, the Bible tells us, are the purposes of marriage: mutual companionship and new lives and new life. To achieve this, the Christian view of marriage recognizes the twin nature of the vows which undergird your marriage. The twin nature vow is this: Marriage is a union of total commitment and of faithfulness. Trust and faithfulness, therefore, are closely related to your love for each other.

And yet, you are not going to maintain these key elements in your marriage alone. A third party is involved in your union here today: our Lord Jesus Christ himself. He is truly present in this church at this moment. Our Lord Jesus Christ is resting his hands on both your shoulders and saying, " NAME and NAME , I am here with you. I am here in your vows to each other. And I will be with you and draw you closer to each other and to me throughout your marriage. I will never leave you nor forsake you."

Those are the words Christ is speaking to you here today, NAME and NAME . He is the resource you will need when your love may flicker and your trust may weaken. He is needed, for your marriage is incomplete until you both live in the atonement found in our Lord Jesus Christ alone.

Now, to *atone* means to be made "at one" again. And Christians are in the business of doing just that with one another. No matter how much common ground there is between you two; no matter how many happy hours you have spent together strolling in the evening or skiing or swimming together; no matter how much you like the same music; no matter how much you are attracted to each other physically, the beauty you see "across a crowded room" becomes modified after marriage. You begin to recognize each other's faults and realize that things are not the way you thought they would be.

To live above with the saints we love,
Ah, that is the purest glory;
To live below with the saints we know,
Ah, that is another story.

(An old Irish ditty, quoted by John Powell in *A Reason to Live! A Reason to Die!*
[Valencia, California: Argus Communications, imprint of Tabor Publishing, 1975],
181)

## Forgiveness

We are all imperfect, sinful human beings. Some things in marriage cannot be cured by talking them out. Some sharp statements or selfish acts cannot be alleviated by therapy. No, there must also be forgiveness. The Christian recognizes that he or she walks every day as a man or woman forgiven by God—forgiven, not because he or she is sincere or of good character, but because God in Christ has absorbed into himself my rebelliousness, my self-centeredness, my wrong-doing, my sin.

Christ died for our sins. And, as God is reconciled to us, let us also be reconciled one to another. This is the strategy of marriage: the strategy of forgiveness, the strategy of being called to be a "little Christ" to our mate, to learn from the very beginning that one of the greatest things we shall be called upon to do in marriage is to forgive each other, in thought, word, and in action. Six words to remember: "Please, forgive me" (not just "I'm sorry" but "Please, forgive me") and "I forgive you."

In summary: The Christian view of marriage recognizes its dual purpose of companionship and the possibility of new lives and new life. It recognizes the twin vows of total commitment and faithfulness. And it recognizes the daily need for forgiveness, the pattern of him who first has forgiven us by dying on the cross, the pattern of Jesus Christ, who loved the world and you and me so much that he gave!

**And so we pray:**

On those who now before you kneel,
O Lord, Thy blessing pour
That each may wake the other's zeal
To love Thee more and more.

Oh, grant them here in peace to live,
In purity and love,
And, this world leaving, to receive
A crown of life above.

(TLH 620:3)

# The "Martyrdom" of Marriage

### Colossians 3:3, [therefore] 13

<u>NAME</u> and <u>NAME</u>,

As a theme for your wedding, I/we have chosen what at first might seem like a very unlikely word: *martyrdom.* The term is not used lightly, for each of you *is* heading into a martyrdom of sorts. In fact, one of the collects in the Orthodox Church at a marriage is for martyrdom.

Ultimately, the only way a marriage will last is when each party martyrs the self for the other, even (as Scripture says, Eph. 5:25) as Christ "gave himself" for the church, for the whole world, in suffering and dying for the sins of humanity on the cross. You are also called, as the Greek word *martyria* means, "to witness to others" this same giving of self for each other.

It is from our Lord that we learn the true nature of marriage. Not that we see our Lord Jesus Christ as a mere example of self-giving to follow. We *can't* emulate him. We are sinners and fail utterly to be the "little Christs" to each other which he daily calls us to be. So we look not on our Lord's martyrdom/self-giving as a model to follow, but rather, devoid of any power of our own, ask for his Holy Spirit to do that in us which we are unable to do. As Scripture says, "God is always at work in you to make you willing and able to obey his own purpose" (Phil. 2:13 TEV). And as our text says, "You died, and your life is now hidden with Christ in God. ... [therefore] ... Bear with each other and forgive whatever grievances you may have against one another."

**Forgiveness**

Therefore, with Christ living in each of you, may your marriage be marked first and foremost of all by the central aspect of Christ's work: forgiveness.

A man had made a fool of himself at a party. The next day he felt complete remorse for his actions and begged his wife to forgive him. "I do, honey," she promised. But the next few months, whenever something came up that displeased the wife, she would bring up the party incident.

"I thought you forgave me for that," the husband said.

"Darling," she responded. "I did forgive you. I just don't want you to forget that I forgave you."

God's forgiveness is not like that. When he forgives, he forgets. Isaiah says, "I, even I, am he who blots out your transgressions, for my own sake, and remembers your sins no more" (Is. 43:25). So also you and I are called to forgive and forget daily. Oh, humanly speaking, we do remember what happened. But God calls us to forgive and not keep on holding against the other person the wrong that happened.

So, forgiveness is the key to your new relationship of marriage, NAME and NAME. We are all imperfect human beings. I'm not talking here about minor imperfections. No, I am speaking of our basic, thoroughly self-centered natures that show up so clearly in the intimacy of marriage. Self always gets in the way. Even if you take a long walk to try to get away from your selfish self, you'll return to find your old self sitting on the doorstep of your marriage.

That's why even the best of Christian marriages requires forgiveness. Each day you and I—all of us here—need to remember that we walk as a man or woman forgiven by God. Not because we're doing a "pretty good job" in being a faithful Christian. Rather, God in Christ has absorbed our sinful selfishness into himself by his death on the cross.

## Costly Grace

Christ died for our sins. Therefore, Scripture enjoins us, as "God was reconciling the world to himself in Christ, not counting men's sins against them [so] he has committed to us the message of reconciliation" (2 Cor. 5:19). There's the divine design for your marriage, NAME and NAME : the plan for forgiveness.

This forgiveness, though, is not an "easy" forgiveness, not "sinning more that grace may abound." Not "cheap grace," but the "costly grace" of Christ. And his holy calling to each of you now is to be a "little Christ," to forgive the other person daily, in thought, word, and in action.

Three words: "Please, forgive me." Not just "I'm sorry" or "I'm sorry you found out" but "Please, forgive me." And then three more words, the more important three in fact: "I forgive you."

When that happens, then, by the daily memory of your Baptism (which Luther said we are to put on like a garment every morning), the Holy Spirit will cause your love to grow. Not just a "love" to be loved. And not only a love for the other person. But more: It will be a love that seeks to capture God's vision of what the other person can become. It will be a self-denying love which by Christ's indwelling strives to enable the other person to become the individual God wants that person to be. To deny yourself may seem like martyrdom, but the results will be exciting and adventurous as you grow closer to each other and closer to the Lord.

May the Lord so bless you. Amen.

# Wearing the Right Clothes

Isaiah 61:10

[I give credit to Ben F. Freudenberg for the germinal idea of the "robes of the Christian," which he used as a children's message. Ushers brought out the various garments from the sacristy.

N.B.: For additional resources, see "The Wedding Sermon," *Concordia Theological Quarterly* 59:1-2 (January–April, 1995) 105-7, by the author.]

"I delight greatly in the LORD; my soul rejoices in my God. For he has clothed me with garments of salvation and arrayed me in a robe of righteousness, as a bridegroom adorns his head like a priest, and as a bride adorns herself with her jewels" (Is. 61:10).

"Garments of salvation" and "a robe of righteousness"— now those are clothes! The clothing you will be wearing when you leave these festivities says something about where you are going and something about your personalities. But the clothes God provides, salvation and righteousness, say even more. They say, "This me and this spouse, this marriage—we belong to the Lord."

When did you first get these spiritual clothes? For most of us it was in the Sacrament of Baptism: "Receive the sign of the holy cross both upon your forehead and upon your heart to mark you as one redeemed by Christ the crucified" (*Lutheran Worship*, 199). You even may have had a white baptismal garment, symbolic of the purity of forgiveness that Christ gives to us through his death and resurrection. "Though your sins are like scarlet, they shall be as white as snow" (Is. 1:18).

Then, later, you were/may have been confirmed. Already a member of the church since Baptism, on confirmation day you made a personal confession of your faith for all to hear. And the Christian congregation again promised nurture for you as you continued your Christian walk. And maybe you wore a special confirmation day dress or a new suit.

And now you are here today wearing [add personalized comments].

But it won't be long and you'll be back in your everyday clothes, NAME wearing _____, and NAME wearing _____.

And then, as weeks of marriage go by, you'll each be in your old clothes. BRIDE'S NAME will see GROOM'S NAME in grubby Levis, unshaved and sweating, working on his car or mowing the lawn. And she'll say, "Did I marry *that?*" And GROOM'S NAME will see BRIDE'S NAME at breakfast, bedraggled and weary. And he will groan, "Whatever happened to the vision I married?" And those old clothes will become reminders that each of you, like all of us, still own our old unspiritual clothes, the clothes of sin.

There will be disappointments, cutting comments, and hurts—and the need to ask forgiveness from each other. And that is the heart of Christian marriage: the forgiveness of sins— of sins one against the other, but most of all, against God.

Scripture calls us to "forgive … so that your Father in heaven may forgive you your sins" (Mark 11:25). "Be kind and compassionate to one another, forgiving each other, just as in Christ God forgave you" (Eph. 4:32). "Bear with each other and forgive whatever grievances you may have against one another. Forgive as the Lord forgave you" (Col. 3:13).

*That* is what the "garment of salvation," the "robe of righteousness" is all about. You are able to forgive because God has forgiven you through Christ's death on the cross. And he empowers you to do so through his Holy Spirit.

Today we rejoice in our God (v. 10)! We ask God for many years of wearing your "garments of salvation." And we all look forward to standing before God's heavenly altar and wearing the crown of life given to those who are "faithful unto death" (Rev. 2:10 RSV).

Therefore, rejoice! As our text says, "I delight greatly in the LORD; my soul rejoices in my God. For he has clothed me with garments of salvation and arrayed me in a robe of righteousness, as a bridegroom adorns his head like a priest, and as a bride adorns herself with her jewels." Amen.

# All We Need to Know About Heaven

1 Thessalonians 4:17

[N.B.: For additional resources, see "Proclaiming Life in Death: The Funeral Sermon," *Concordia Theological Quarterly* 58:1 (January 1994) 5–24, by the author.]

There is reference in the Bible to one man who never died. His name was Enoch. Scripture says God translated him directly from life on earth to being in the presence of God in heaven.

A little girl was once asked to tell the story of Enoch. She said, "Well, Enoch and God were good friends. And they used to take long walks in Enoch's garden. One day God said, 'Enoch, you look tired. Why don't you come into my place and stay and rest awhile?' And so he did." In a sense, we can say that God said the same thing to NAME: "NAME, you look very tired. Why don't you come to my place and stay and rest?" (Source unknown)

That poetic way of looking at NAME's passing away from our presence may comfort us. But we do not say that God *caused* NAME's death. Well-meaning people say "God called him/her home" or, "God took him/her." But God does not cause death; we do, for we are all mortal, all sinners.

Death comes upon us all because of our sinful condition— our sins of commission and omission which place our *selves* first and God last. Sin is just that: self-absorption and self-centeredness. Sin is ignoring God and planning our lives as if he did not exist. It is having a meager prayer life or no prayer life at all. It is having little to do with Christ's church on earth—fallible as we all admit the church is as an institution. Sin is ignoring our Baptism, by which we were forgiven our sins by the gracious redemptive power of God's Holy Spirit. Sin is staying away from Holy Communion, where we receive Christ's body and blood for the forgiveness of our sin. In sum, sin is living one's life independent from God.

A memorial service concerns not just the dead, but the living. God calls us all—people in the church and outside it—to repentance. We have a gracious God who does not desire our punishment and death, but who sent his only beloved Son into the world to suffer and die on the cross for our sins. The payment for our sin cost him the life of his Son, our Savior. But by Christ's death and resurrection we are forgiven people. God declares us righteous—made right again in his eyes—through Christ's atoning work for us. We cannot save ourselves. Christ did. And he wants the assurance and peace and comfort and hope of that forgiveness to be a living reality in our daily lives. God says, "I have engraved you on the palms of my hands" (Is. 49:16). "I have redeemed you … you are mine" (Is. 43:1). NAME believed that. He/she was baptized and knew he/she was a forgiven child of God.

[Here personalize recent events in the deceased's life that witnessed to his or her faith in Jesus Christ.]

We need to know only three words about NAME's state right now. The words are "with the Lord" (1 Thess. 4:17). That's what life eternal is: being in the loving, personal presence of God himself. Nothing can be more wonderful. We here today are human, and we sorrow at losing NAME . But NAME would not have us grieve, for he/she is "with the Lord!"

Imagine if [spouse's name, if living] were going through all of NAME's papers and found a letter from him/her which went like this:

> A final letter to my family. When I die, please do not grieve for me. I am beyond pain. By God's grace, I am in the presence of our Lord. You are the ones in pain. That grieves me as I write this, but in heaven I will not know pain.
>
> So if you hurt, I am truly sorry. But dwell on the joys—the many joyful times God permitted us to have together. God has been most merciful and gracious to us!

Remember our common faith in our Lord and Savior Jesus Christ. He lives in our hearts. Think of me too as living in your hearts.

So do not sorrow as those who have no hope; I will see you again. So rejoice! Christ died for us—and rose again! And because of that, I will see you again!" (Adapted from *The Bright Red Sports Car*, 67-68)

 NAME  is at peace. Let us too be at peace. And let us find our comfort in him alone who gives solace in our grief: Jesus Christ, who forgives us all our sins and seals to us the sure and certain hope of life eternal.

# And Bid Her Welcome Home

## 1 Corinthians 15:55

 NAME  is with the Lord. What a blessing he/she has this very minute, being in the living presence of Christ, our Savior and Redeemer! Today we mourn his/her death. We will see him/her no more on this earth. But  NAME  was prepared for his/her death.

[Here insert personal references from the deceased's life that lead you to the conviction of his/her faith in Christ Jesus.]

Yes, we mourn his/her death, but we also celebrate his/her ascension into heaven.

Some churches use a Paschal candle, which they light on Easter Eve and don't extinguish until Ascension Day, when Christ left our vision and ascended into heaven. Even as the Paschal candle is snuffed out to show a passage to heaven, so NAME's life was snuffed out. A miracle has happened. As the hymn says,

> A moment's space, and gently, wondrously,
> Released from earthly ties,
> Elijah's chariot bears her [the soul] up to thee,
> Thro' all these lower skies
> To yonder shining regions,
> While down to meet her come
> The blessed angel legions
> And bid her welcome home.
> (TLH 619:3)

Yes,  NAME  is in heaven now—with the Lord. That's all we need to know. But, humanly speaking, we still miss him/her sorely and ask questions at his/her death. For one thing, beyond the relief that we all feel for him/her, that there is no more pain, suffering, and discomfort, we wonder what his/her existence is like now.

## The Friend Who Is There

I personally cannot tell you anything about the life to come, for I have never been there. But I have a friend who is there. And I trust that friend. Our Savior said, "I am the resurrection and the life. He who believes in me will live, even though he dies; and whoever lives and believes in me will never die" (John 11:25–26).

"Marvel not at this: for the hour is coming, in which all that are in the graves shall hear his voice, and shall come forth; they that have done good, unto the resurrection of life; and they that have done evil, unto the resurrection of damnation" (John 5:28–29 KJV).

"Do not let your hearts be troubled. Trust in God; trust also in me. In my Father's house are many rooms; if it were not so, I would have told you. I am going there to prepare a place for you. And if I go and prepare a place for you, I will come back and take you to be with me that you also may be where I am" (John 14:1–3).

"I have told you these things, so that in me you may have peace. In this world you will have trouble. But take heart! I have overcome the world" (John 16:33).

Therefore, with promises like these from Christ, we are able to say, "O death, where is thy sting? O grave, where is thy victory?" (1 Cor. 15:55 KJV).

## No Fear of Death

We do not fear death, for it is only a doorway into the presence of the Father. We do not fear the grave, for it has no power over us. Our victory is in our Lord Jesus Christ, who has forgiven us and forever freed us from our sins by his death and resurrection and made us citizens of his kingdom into all eternity.

That is what death meant to  NAME : victory! His/her certain hope was that of the Apostle Paul: "I desire to depart and be with Christ, which is better by far" (Phil. 1:23).

Those words aptly express our feelings as Christians today

as well as our human inability to understand the mysteries of life and death. As Paul also said, "For now we see through a glass, darkly; but then face to face: now I know in part; but then shall I know even as also I am known" (1 Cor. 13:12 KJV). Even as we now mourn the departed, he/she is already in complete happiness and bliss—he/she has already seen our Savior face to face and is no longer aware of the sorrows of earth left behind.

Since there is no "time" in eternity, it's really no time at all until the family will be fully reunited in heaven with him/her. Then you will not "see through a glass, darkly," but you too, will see face to face. Until that time, we are content, we "rest in the Lord," in the knowledge that this death is swallowed up in victory. For we know that this death had no ultimate sting, that the grave holds no victory, for  NAME  was faithful unto death and now has received the crown of life.

## Abide with Me

"Abide with me," we pray in one hymn to our Lord. But that's also our Lord's invitation to us. "My Father's house has plenty of room; come in and abide with me. Join me at the heavenly banquet, where there are no more tears or hunger or thirst. Come, you who are blessed by my Father; abide with me."

This voice of God, which gives the peace that the world cannot give, should calm any questions in our minds. Instead, together with  NAME  and the apostle Paul—both in glory now—we rejoice.

> Oh, the depth of the riches both of the wisdom and knowledge of God! How unsearchable *are* His judgments and His ways past finding out! *"For who has known the mind of the LORD? Or who has become His counselor? Or who has first given to Him And it shall be repaid to him?"* For of Him and through Him and to Him *are* all things, to whom *be* glory forever" (Rom. 11:33–36 NKJV).

## With the Lord

These things, then, we affirm today. That he/she is with the Lord. That through his/her Baptism he/she, has been "buried with [Christ] through Baptism into death, that just as Christ was raised from the dead by the glory of the Father" (Rom. 6:4 NKJV), so he/she too—in the mystery of the timelessness of eternity—has risen to the life above and is in the presence of the Lord.

We mourn NAME's death today. He/she will be missed, to be sure. But this service today is not for the dead but for the living. Knowing that NAME has his/her victory and is with the Lord, forever out of pain and suffering, we have the task of comforting one another in the pain of separation. We have a "sermon" to say to one another about our own day of death—whether that comes on the freeway driving home or years from now. Our message to one another: "Remember who you are and whose you are and where you came from and where you are going in the Lord."

May each of you live as a "little Christ" for whatever period of days remain for you on this island colony called earth. And may the peace that God alone gives, and which NAME now has, in its fullest radiance and abundance, be yours.

May the peace of God, which passes all human understanding, keep your hearts and minds through faith in Christ Jesus.

# Gone but Not Lost

1 Thessalonians 4:13a, 17b

[Some of the material is from *At Life's End.*]

We do not want you to be ignorant about those who fall asleep …
we will be with the Lord forever. (Text)

A little girl, whose baby brother had just died, asked her
mother where the baby had gone. Her mother replied, "To be
with Jesus." A few days later, talking to a friend, the mother said,
"I am so grieved to have lost my baby."

The little girl heard her and, remembering what her mother
had told her, looked up to her and asked, "Mommy, is a thing
lost when you know where it is?"

"No, of course not."

"Well, then," she replied, "How can baby be lost when he
has gone to be with Jesus?" (*At the Death of a Child,* 17)

**With the Lord**

NAME has died, but he/she is not lost. We know where
NAME is. NAME is "with the Lord!" That's what everlasting life
is: being in the loving, personal presence of God himself.
Nothing can be more wonderful, and nothing can be more
comforting than that.

From Scripture we know also that we will be different in
heaven. As the apostle Paul notes in 1 Corinthians 15:40-44,
on earth we have a physical body; there we will have a spiritual body. From our limited perspective, like looking through a
darkened glass, we cannot really comprehend what the spiritual body will be like. Yet we are assured that in heaven we shall
fully "know" each other (see 1 Cor. 13:9-10, 12). We will visibly
recognize others in heaven. This is demonstrated a number of
times in Scripture. For example, at the transfiguration, the disciples recognized Moses and Elijah even though they had never

seen them before (Matt. 17:4). Therefore, be reassured that you will see and recognize "face to face" NAME as well as all who have died as Christians. Ours is a great God, who makes this joyous event possible for us.

> Apostles, martyrs, prophets, there
> Around my Savior stand;
> And soon my friends in Christ below
> Will join the glorious band.
> (TLH 618:4)

Also, because there is no time or "waiting" in eternity, from our *human* perspective, NAME here, who died "in the Lord," is in heaven ready to greet you. Although you are separated temporarily from your loved ones on earth, when you die it will be only "the twinkling of an eye" (1 Cor. 15:52) before you are reunited in heaven with those who have been "faithful unto death" (Rev. 2:10 KJV) to our Lord Jesus Christ.

Indeed, as Scripture affirms in Ephesians 2:6 (KJV), being "raised ... up together" at the resurrection, you will "sit together in heavenly places in Christ Jesus."

What a reunion that will be!

> There I shall dwell forever,
> No more a parting guest,
> With all Thy blood-bought children
> In everlasting rest,
> The pilgrim toils forgotten,
> The pilgrim conflicts o'er,
> All earthly griefs behind me,
> Eternal joys before.
> (TLH 586:7)

## Forever with the Lord

Comforted with this knowledge, that we will see NAME face to face again, you and I are now called to live in a certain way here today. Yes, we will come to the end of our life, but as Christians we need not fear death. For it is only the doorway into the loving presence of God, our heavenly Father. It is not a "leap into the dark" but a "welcome home" into the arms of the one who first created us and has loved us from our mothers' wombs. He is the one who first gave us the forgiveness of all our sins by the washing and regeneration in Holy Baptism. He is the one who has nurtured us through his "means of grace" throughout our lives.

Therefore, we need not live with anxiety. We know that our eternal life, in which we already live through Baptism, is assured through Christ's death and resurrection *for us* and all human beings who believe in him. "Because I live, you also will live" (John 14:19). Yes, Christ is the way to die, for he is "the way, the truth, and the life" (John 14:6 KJV).

As a result, you and I live daily in hope—not that we hope we'll be saved, for we *are* saved by God's grace. Rather, we live with the biblical understanding of the word *hope:* the confidence and conviction that when we die we shall be forever "with the Lord."

Do you believe this about your own death and the life to come? God wants you to be certain, for he tells us in Scripture:

> God is love, and whoever lives in love lives in God and God lives in him. Love is made perfect in us in order that we may have courage on the Judgment Day; and we will have it because our life in this world is the same as Christ's. There is no fear in love; perfect love drives out all fear. So then, love has not been made perfect in anyone who is afraid, because fear has to do with punishment. We love because God first loved us (1 John 4:16–19 TEV).

Knowing that God is love and that he freely gives us the forgiveness of sins and his love through his Son, why should we fear? If we fear at all, it might be because we're not hooked into the channels of his love. The point is, keep connected to God's holy Word and Sacraments, for our love *is* imperfect and will not be fully perfected until we are in heaven. Keep in mind that the victory over death has already been won for us by the life, death, resurrection, and ascension of Jesus Christ. The question you and I are called to ask ourselves each day is, Am I, by the power of God's Holy Spirit, daily living in that victory? Am I fully at peace with God and prepared for my death?

Daily God calls us to repent of our sins and to trust completely in Christ for all that we need in this life and the life to come.

> Seek the LORD while he may be found; call on him while he is near. Let the wicked forsake his way and the evil man his thoughts. Let him turn to the LORD, and he will have mercy on him, and to our God, for he will freely pardon (Is. 55:6–7).

And God's promise will be fulfilled in you:

> Those who hope in the LORD will renew their strength. They will soar on wings like eagles; they will run and not grow weary, they will walk and not be faint (Is. 40:31).

And the words of our Lord will ring in your ears:

> Come, you who are blessed by my Father; take your inheritance, the kingdom prepared for you since the creation of the world (Matt. 25:34).

And:

> Well done, good and faithful servant! You have been faithful with a few things; I will put you in charge of many things. Come and share your master's happiness! (Matt. 25:23)

NAME is now "with the Lord." And we will see NAME again. Until that day comes, Christ calls you and me to live each day for itself, but in the joyous certainty of our resurrection.

"Thanks be to God! He gives us the victory through our Lord Jesus Christ" (1 Cor. 15:57).

# The Keys of the Kingdom

## Matthew 16:18-19

[For much of this material I am indebted to my sainted friend Robert K. Menzel, (†) 1989. Some aspects of the two sets of principles in the conclusion were adapted from Carl Walter Berner, *Spiritual Power for Your Congregation* (St. Louis: Concordia Publishing House, 1956), 90–93.]

Imagine several months have passed since this joyous festival service. Your newly installed Pastor  NAME  has been preaching the Gospel faithfully. And there have been new visitors to the church. One day two agnostics, non-believers, are walking by the church and one says to the other, "I see you've gone and heard that guy preach several times. You don't believe that stuff, do you?"

And the other fellow replies, "No, but he does."

Do you think that conversation could happen? I certainly do, for the pastor being ordained (installed) here today is a man of conviction. And he will be preaching the Word of God with boldness and power. It is that power which I want to talk about briefly today: the power given to a Christian congregation, and the power the members entrust to you,  NAME , their pastor. It is the power that comes from God alone and that is referred to in one of our older introits: "Behold the Lord, the Ruler has come; and the kingdom and the power and the glory are in his hand" (Epiphany, *TLH*).

This power is symbolized in our text as "the keys of the kingdom of heaven." Yes, our blessed Lord has the keys of the kingdom in his hand, even as he came to the apostle John in the book of Revelation and said, "Fear not; I am the first and the last: I am he that liveth, and was dead; and, behold, I am alive for evermore ... and have the keys of hell and of death" (Rev. 1:17–18 KJV).

Only God could make a statement like that. Yet this creator

of life, the author of the universe, humbled himself, and became Representative Man—and died. Just think of that—the Almighty God stepped down from his throne on high, assumed human form, took upon himself our sin and guilt, and by his death on the cross made atonement for the sins of the whole human race. Yes, Christ died. But he also conquered death, and he lives and reigns to all eternity. And in his hands, he says, "I have the keys of death and hell. I am able to consign men to eternal death because of their sins—or, I am able to free them from death and hell." His keys are the forgiveness of sins. As Scripture says, "Sin *pays* its servants: the wage is death. But God *gives* to those who serve him: his free gift is eternal life through Jesus Christ our Lord" (Rom. 6:23 JBP).

## The Passing of the Keys

But now let me tell you something that, if you heard it for the first time, would be absolutely incredible. These keys which Christ has in his hands, these keys that open and close the gates of hell, that open and shut the portals of heaven, keys that the Lord of lords alone possesses—these keys he has given to you, <u>CONGREGATION NAME</u> Church. Christ said, "All power is given unto me in heaven and in earth" (Matt. 28:18 KJV). Or, as the RSV has it, "All authority…has been given to me." With this authority Christ has delegated the power of these keys to you here on the earth. Here in our text he gave it to Peter as the spokesman of all the disciples; again he gave it to the 12 disciples; and still again he gave it to the little congregation assembled in the upper room on Easter Eve when he appeared to them with the blessing "Peace be to you." Three times he spoke the words, and three times he passed on the keys, "I will give you the keys of the kingdom of heaven, and whatever you bind on earth will be bound in heaven, and whatever you loose on earth will be loosed in heaven" (Matt. 16:19 NKJV). Or, as another passage has it, "Whose soever sins ye remit, they are remitted unto them; and whose soever sins ye retain, they are retained" (John 20:23 KJV).

How long has it been since you have read the fifth Chief Part of Luther's Small Catechism? The Office of the Keys is the power, the authority, to preach the Word and administer the Sacraments, the power to forgive and retain sins. This means that you—the church of God—are to forgive the sins of the penitent and open the doors of heaven to them; and you are to retain the sins of the impenitent and close the door of heaven to them as long as they do not repent.

These are the keys in your hands. This is the power which our blessed Lord has given you. It's really amazing when we think of how weak and frail and unworthy we are! Yet you have the keys of the kingdom, "even though," as Luther says, "all of you were but stable boys." Of course, you can't all crowd into this chancel to speak the comforting, heaven-opening words of absolution in the Holy Eucharist; you can't all squeeze into this pulpit to preach the precious Gospel; you can't all dip your hands into the water of the baptismal font and pour its regenerating water on an infant's brow; you can't all offer the bread and wine to penitents kneeling at this altar in Holy Communion. Nor have you all been called by this congregation to do so.

But one has been called and trained to do so, one who holds fast the faithful Word as he has been taught, one who is able by sound doctrine to exhort and convince. In his hand you are placing the keys of the kingdom to be used among you.

This is what you are doing today, as you, CONGREGATION NAME Church, confirm the solemn call extended to NAME to be your pastor. In your name the pastor will do that which is the right and responsibility of you all: the opening of the door of heaven with the keys—with the saving Gospel, the cleansing Sacraments, and the comfort-giving absolution.

And yet, properly understood, it is not you who have called Pastor NAME. It is God, who through you has called this man to serve here. Otherwise, by what right can any pastor stand before others and say, "I forgive you all your sins" and "Repent and believe the Gospel" when he dips a hand in baptismal water or lifts a cup of communion wine to your lips? It is not because this person is better than his fellows. It is because God has called him through you. Through you, God whispered to him and conscripted his service to administer the keys of the kingdom of heaven.

**Two Keys**

Our blessed Lord gave two keys to you, the Christian congregation, and you are entrusting them to your pastor. One key is to enlarge the church, the other to keep it pure. On one key is written "Use this to win." On the other is written "Use this to warn." Jesus wants you to use both of them faithfully.

The key to win is the "Opening Key." You—pastor and congregation together—will be using it as long as you keep the preaching of the Gospel as the central focus in the program of CONGREGATION NAME Church, as long as you develop a greater appreciation of the Sacrament of the Altar, as long as you derive still greater meaning from your Baptism, and use absolution in a meaningful way. You will be using the opening key by your witness and worship in the home, by the Sunday school and Bible classes here, by your support of radio and television ministries, by the work of our church in foreign lands, and by your own personal testimony to the Gospel. In these ways, "whatever you loose on earth will be loosed in heaven."

On the other hand, there is the key to warn—not only to warn unbelievers to repent and prepare for Christ's return but also to lovingly warn one another that we are not just to go through the motions and the routines of our worship while our hearts really are somewhere else. Yes, the key to warn is also to be used in a Christian congregation, lest these words of Scripture apply to it: "These people draw near to Me with their mouth, And honor Me with their lips, But their heart is far from Me" (Matt. 15:8 NKJV).

54

## The Ideal Pastor

How very important that pastor and people have the right relationship as they do this together! Some congregations have a completely wrong attitude towards their pastor. They either expect too much of the pastor or else they expect the wrong thing. For example, one congregation, in calling a new pastor, made the following list of qualifications:

> He should be energetic and enterprising, yet ripe in experience and wisdom. Not under 40 nor over 45. Married, with a wife who is anxious to help, and must be neither too good looking nor too homely, and neither too fat nor too thin. He should not be bound to the forms of either high church or low. He should be a good preacher, able to put across his message eloquently and briefly. Devout, yet broad-minded. An inspiration to the flock, but just a bit thick-skinned.

Of such a set of qualifications, one person said, "All that congregation wants is an earthly saint!"

That's like another congregation that wanted its pastor to be 1) born in Bethlehem; 2) work for nothing; and 3) stay forever.

No, a Christian congregation needs to recognize the limitations of its pastor, who, after all, is a human being. And one of the quickest ways to deny the priesthood of all believers is to promote the heresy that everything in the life of the church depends on the minister. A parish needs to recognize that in giving the keys of the kingdom to its pastor, it does not absolve itself of its necessary Christian work of serving—what we might call "the priesthood of all believers." The congregation still bears the keys. And the way in which you use these keys in this congregation depends on your attitude towards the office of the ministry and towards your pastor. Permit me to suggest some guidelines as to how you, the bearers of the keys, are to regard this pastor whom you are entrusting with the keys.

## Pastor and People

To you, _CONGREGATION NAME_ Church, here are loving responses to the Gospel as you begin to work with your new pastor.

1. First of all, trust confidently that your pastor, as a faithful steward, will always try to do everything to the glory of the Savior and for the best interests of _CONGREGATION NAME_ Church.

2. Remember that the pastor is a special target for the devil's arrows. His Achilles' heels are pride and fear. So, with your prayers build a strong wall of defense around the pastor.

3. Ask God for an extra measure of His Spirit for your pastor, that the pastor might have courage to speak the Law fearlessly and the Gospel winsomely.

4. Do not expect your pastor to rely on visions or dreams to know when your loved ones are sick or in distress. The pastor cannot apply the keys of the kingdom to those whose needs are not known.

5. Your pastor is not perfect or infallible. For the most part, overlook any failings he may have and look into the mirror to see if your weaknesses are not at least sometimes greater in size and number. If some fault appears to be serious, tell him about it in a loving way. You will find him responsive.

6. Do not judge the pastor's motives or think unkindly about him on the basis of hearsay. Do not expect to hear only good things about the pastor, for even the Lord Jesus did not please everybody, especially not those whom he rebuked because of their sins.

7. Don't tie down your pastor with all kinds of red tape, like the giant in _Gulliver's Travels._ Take responsibility for some tasks yourselves so that the pastor might be freed for the central task of ministry: the care of souls.

8. Finally, give the pastor and his family the full benefit of your friendship and your love.

And you, pastor elect:

1. "Preach the Word! Be ready in season *and* out of season. Convince, rebuke, exhort, with all longsuffering and teaching" (2 Tim. 4:2 NKJV).

Oh, there will be those who will say to you:

> Preach about the other man, preacher,
> The man we all can see—
> The man who drinks and beats his wife,
> The man who swears and raises strife.
> Preach about the other man, preacher,
> Don't preach about me.
> (Source unknown)

People may say that to you, but it is your responsibility to preach the Law and the Gospel clearly, "rightly dividing the Word of Truth."

2. Remember, further, that people do not come to hear you but the Word of God. They sing, "Blessed Jesus at Thy Word, we are gathered all to hear *thee*." So make Christ the center of your preaching, and may it be empowered by love: "We love Him, because He first loved us"; and, "Beloved, if God so loved us, we also ought to love one another" (1 John 4:19, 11 NKJV).

3. And, through it all, may God the Holy Spirit grant you the grace to live a life of Christ-centered conduct.

And as both of you, congregation and pastor, seek to use these keys of the kingdom in keeping with our Lord's will, may you remember that in the Office of the Keys you have the very power of heaven itself, the "power of God unto salvation to everyone that believes," the power of *your* salvation. May you join the multitudes that see it and marvel and glorify God, who has given such power to human beings. Yes, even to you!

# Are You a Tame Captive of Your Community?

Romans 12:2

[Some of this material is adapted from an address to mission developers in Los Angeles by Robert K. Menzel.]

"Don't let the world around you squeeze you into its own mould, but let God re-mould your minds from within, so that you may prove in practice that the Plan of God for you is good, meets all his demands and moves towards the goal of true maturity" (Rom. 12:2 *Letters*).

Welcome to <u>Congregation Name</u> Church. Welcome to <u>City and State Name</u>, USA.

Picture a family settling down in this community. As the family selects a grocery store and meets the neighbors, it looks over here and sees the spire of <u>Congregation Name</u> Church. What will this family see?

Will they see a church which is true to its name: <u>Congregation Name</u> Church? Will they see a church true to its heritage, holding true and sharing freely the pure Word of God and the blessed sacraments? Will they see a church continuing in the things it has learned and has been assured of in the years of its blessed history, knowing of whom it learned them (2 Tim. 3:14)? Or will they see a church exposed and succumbed to the cult of comfort and conformity in the modern community around it? As Stanley Rowland has put it, today "the house of the Lord [has often been reduced] to a comfort station." With few exceptions, the suburban church has become the tame captive of its community. Is this what they will see?

This is what the Apostle Paul warns us against in the text I have chosen for this service, a joyful worship of thanksgiving in which you dedicate your new house of worship (or, celebrate your church's anniversary). Paul says, "Don't let the world around you squeeze you into its own mould, but let God re-mould your minds from within."

## Remolded from Within

A new chapter in a new book has opened for your church. And it is my challenge to you [theme] that this ministry first of all not be molded by the world around it, but that your ministry remold the community from within by bearing clear witness to the living Savior, in whom alone this community can find salvation from sin, peace with God, and purpose for life.

This is particularly important because the new family coming to this area will hardly find the true Christian faith emulated on the block in which they live. Popular guides to confident living and paperbacks urging "self-help" are much more in vogue than the old "lamp and light," the sacred Word of God. The barbecue table is much more popular than the communion table. TV, the altar of American culture, receives much more attention than the family altar. And the house of our Lord is too often a foreign land to the home owner whose glory is the garden and whose god is a patio.

But if  CONGREGATION NAME  Church continues to let God "re-mould its mind from within" with the blessed Word of God and the sacraments, then it can meet the challenge of the modern American community here in  CITY NAME. For CONGREGATION NAME  Church can well be the mother-church for the future missions to be established in this niche of the Lord's Vineyard, as the glittering fruits of technology continue to tumble over the countryside and as new industry rises in concrete and steel from the erstwhile pastureland. Nineteen centuries ago the home-missions board of First Christian Church in Antioch sent out a missionary who had just gotten a little congregation off to a good start in Philippi. He had left a Roman jailer and his family and a widowed weaver and her kin in charge of the new mission there. Then he came to Thessalonica. Once he had the ears of folks there, he "argued with them from the scriptures, explaining and quoting passages to prove the necessity for the death of Christ and his rising again from the dead" (Acts 17:2–3 JBP). The writer of this bit of history notes that this kind of ministry netted results, "Some of them were convinced and sided with Paul" (v. 4, JBP).

This is the ministry to which God has called this congregation. Just arguing won't challenge or win this community, but "explaining and quoting passages to prove the necessity for the death of Christ and his rising again from the dead" will! Yes, this is the message of Christ's [the Lutheran] Church. We call ourselves *Lutherans* because God used blessed Martin Luther almost 500 years ago to bring us back to the book which alone has a message of hope for man. We are proud of Martin Luther, the "man with the book," as he was called. But we are much more concerned about the "book with the Man," the Man Jesus Christ, who alone is our message for the contemporary community. The impact of *this* book [the Bible] upon modern man lies in the Person to whom it gives primary and persuasive witness: Jesus. A Scripture-grounded ministry is a Christ-centered ministry. Truly scriptural preaching and teaching finds the cross in the middle. The arrows of Old Testament prophecy point forward to it. And the shadow of the cross is cast across every page of the New.

In Scripture we see the heartwarming story of a mighty and majestic God who, however, humbled himself by taking a "great dive" to earth and becoming Representative Man to die for us that we, through the "leap of faith" in this great God-Man, might again have fellowship with our Creator. The people of the modern community, however, hardly take note of the gist of the Gospel. The concepts of *salvation* and *redemption* are irrelevant to them, for these ideas seem so sticky, nonactive, and old-fashioned. Pseudo-sophisticated people often react like the little boy in Robert Grave's poem "The Boy Out of Church" (John Bartlett, *Familiar Quotations* [Boston: Little, Brown and

Company, thirteenth edition 1955], 972):

 I do not like the Sabbath,
The soapsuds and the starch,
The troops of solemn people
Who to Salvation march.

## Tame Captives?

We need to use some vigorously and decisively applied Law to show Mr. And Mrs. Community that they are not really free out there in the open air. Rather they are trapped, as David Roberts points out, by "nothing less than a creeping, totalitarian religion ... [that] dictates how a person shall find security, self-esteem, standards of value, and reasons for living." And the question you and I have to ask ourselves is to what extent we personally have become tame captives of our secular community—and its self-centered values. How much have we let our pagan surroundings squeeze us into the mold of its false values?

True Christianity will continue to seem irrelevant as long as it is simply identified with "going to heaven" while we have it so good here on earth. Salvation does include going to heaven, but it also means the freedom-right-now that God gives through the free and freeing act of salvation, Jesus Christ—the only free thing in this inflated age. Christ is the way out of earth and into heaven. But he is also the way out of the squirrel cage of materialistic, glittery, chromium-plated self-centeredness and into the many mansions of salvation which are ours in Christ.

Nothing less than a Christ-centered ministry will challenge the people of this community. And after Christ's Gospel brings them in, you will need God's own remolding process to build them up: his sacred Word and sacraments. Those who come to this church need to learn that church is not just another branch of the Rotary Club. They must see that the saints who call themselves members of this parish are really "proving in practice" (as our text says) "that the Plan of God for [them] is good, meets all his demands and moves towards the goal of true maturity." The plans and pressures and publicities of today must not be the only thing that attracts them, or like all quick-charge methods that build up the voltage too quickly, the whole works will be damaged in the long run. Rather, there must be an ongoing program of Word and sacrament so that you "don't let the world squeeze you into its own mould, but let God re-mould your minds from within." Nor will it work to rely on the "osmosis" method in the hope that some little drop of dedicated Christianity may soak through into these people just by getting together in the sanctified shelter of this ultra-modern building. Nor will perennial patience and pious plati-tudes win the modern American community. Mute coexistence is not the program of the church of Jesus Christ. This church has a message. This church has a witness to make. And if it doesn't, the witness of the world will press the church, and the church will soon find itself being squeezed into the world's own mould.

So this is no small task for you, the dedicated people and pastor of  CONGREGATION NAME  Church, to let God continue to re-mold you from within, to keep your eyes on that Cross. But if you do, one pair of eyes after another in this community will follow your gaze. And then the Spirit of Christ will capture other hearts and hands for our Savior's Kingdom too. When Christ's cross—and its meaning, the forgiveness of sins and sal-vation of blood-bought souls by the God-Man Jesus Christ—is kept central in the thoughts and program of the members of this church, then  CONGREGATION NAME  Church will fulfill its ministry, and the Words of our Lord will be fulfilled, "If I am lift-ed up …, I will draw all men to myself" (John 12:32 JBP).

**Taking the Community Captive**

Now let's see how the very qualities which characterize the community here can be turned to a good end in bringing people into contact and a living relationship with the body of

Christ. As we have said, the church need not be the tame captive of its community. The very qualities (or drawbacks) that characterize life here may be turned into great advantages to the church. For this community is not so much a place as a state of mind.

## The Drive for Advancement

One thing that characterizes this community is the drive for advancement. This area is populated with people on the go, and the direction they are headed is up. Unfortunately, success is not always measured in terms of skill or service, but in advancement with corresponding pay increases. Getting a raise seems to be the real meaning of work. That same standard of value begins to color one's whole way of living. People put up with living in a small house until the family income will permit purchase of a swankier one. And this whole moving-up process, with its sense of here today and gone tomorrow, causes a fragmentation of commitments which in turn makes long-lasting involvement with the church difficult.

These dangers for the church, however, can be turned into genuine *opportunities* for the church as it is challenged by the modern community. Such people on the go are a potential work force that can pour new dynamic and energy into the leadership of Christ's kingdom. Those who want advancement can find it in the kingdom of God. They also can find an intellectual and spiritual advancement, assuming we help them see that their Sunday school idea of the church needs to mature spiritually. Those who want a vital, challenging faith will find themselves fighting an uphill battle! And that's just fine! That is the time when the kingdom is best and bravest and strongest: when the battle is uphill. It is advancement in the knowledge and love of Jesus Christ. Nineteen centuries of Christendom have proved that.

So, if you, as Scripture says, are set on "equipping the saints for their work of serving, that the entire body might be edified," then you will elevate and sanctify people in their avid search for cultural and religious identification. You will help them (as our text says) "move toward the goal of true maturity." For your kind of fellowship in the Gospel will transpose the people who assemble in this multi-purpose building from being a mere "group" in this community into becoming a congregation vitally conscious of its incorporation into the mystical and wondrous body of Christ!

## The Family

A second trend in the community is that amid all the tensions and insecurity and mobility of life, many people find security in (as they put it) "the kids." "The best of everything for the kids; nothing is too good for them." More than a few families are joining churches "for the sake of the children." Here again our churches are to learn from the New Testament. The apostle Paul thought in terms of family life. How often we read, "And they were baptized, and their house." It is high time that the worth of the Sunday schools be determined, not by the number of squirming small fry we can squeeze into every nook and cranny of our already-too-small first unit, but in terms of *families* won for Christ and his church.

Whether they are straying, former church members who need to be reclaimed or people who have never heard the precious story of the death and resurrection of Christ, the question is, What are we doing for their families? That is the question to ask. This church has a high and holy responsibility to establish Christian training *in the family,* which does a far better job of training than does the church or the school.

## Gossip

A third characteristic of community which the church can use to serve our Lord's ends is, strangely, gossip. The beauty of your church may bring many visitors into these pews. But you are not to be satisfied with easy pickings. Learn a lesson from the newsmongers on your block and apply it in a wholesome way to the mission of your church to this community.

You are familiar with the chit-chat that occurs in the supermarket, a "did-you-hear-this" or "did-you-hear that" commentary about the fellow down the street with the new lawn mower or new car or new wife. Well, gossip and Gospel are cousins, we are told. Etymologically and characteristically, Mr. And Mrs. Church Member in  CITY NAME  will gossip about, talk about, not just the neighbors but also about the most important person: the Savior. When St. Paul looked back many years later on the fruits of his ministry in Thessalonica, he could say, "You have become a sort of sounding-board from which the Word of the Lord has rung out" (1 Thess. 1:8 JBP). In other words, those people who have found meaning for time and eternity in the indwelling Christ will tell their neighbors, who are in a haunted search for meaning in life, that it is found at the cross and the open tomb of the risen Savior.

There you have it. As you by God's grace enjoy the blessing of this church, may you be ready to accept the challenge of the modern community and to fling back the challenge of the atonement and resurrection of Jesus Christ. In this community's "drive for advancement," its "everything for the kids," and its good-natured gossip, may you superimpose the "good plan" of the Lord Jesus Christ into the life of each family that lives within sight of this beckoning spire. The challenge of CONGREGATION NAME  Church to the community is going to be found in the faith and hope and love of this little "community-in-love"—a God-given, Christ-centered, Spirit-impelled love.

Oh, your faith and love will mean hard work; your hope in the Lord Jesus Christ will mean sheer dogged endurance. Do not let up in your efforts, for a prophetic voice is needed. Keep before you the challenge the community is presenting to you. And meet this challenge with the precious Gospel of our blessed Lord. When you do, you will be fulfilling the advice of the Apostle in our text, when he says, "Don't let the world around you squeeze you into its own mould, but let God re-mould your minds from within, so that you may prove in practice that the Plan of God for you is good, meets all his demands and moves towards the goal of true maturity."

# It's Not Wrong to Be Rich

Mark 12:30

A layman was making a call on a wealthy businessman, asking him to help in the Lord's work. The man wrote a check for $250 and handed it to him. Just then someone in his office brought in a message. The businessman read it with dismay.

"This message tells me I have just suffered a great loss," he said. "It makes a great difference in my affairs. I shall have to write you another check."

"I understand," said the layman and handed back the check for $250.

The businessman's checkbook was still open. He wrote another check and handed it to the layman, who read it with amazement.

"But this check is for $1,000," he gasped. "Haven't you made a mistake?"

"No," said the businessman. "That message was really from God. It read, 'Do not lay up for yourselves treasures on earth.' " (*Seasonal Illustrations,* 132)

Would you have acted the way that man did? Often we have lost our focus on what living—and dying—is all about.

We have lost the proper perspective on the use of our possessions, our money—indeed, at times we have lost the right vision of what it means to be a Christian.

Our text says, "You shall love the LORD your God with all your heart, with all your soul, with all your mind, and with all your strength" (NKJV).

Thus, the theme for my message on this Stewardship Sunday is: <u>Although we are often curved in on ourselves and make only partial commitment to our Lord, he calls us to die to self and to give our total dedication to him.</u>

## We Don't Want Your Money

Picture yourself in the divine service of one of our Asian churches in a major metropolitan area. At the time for the offering, the pastor arises and quietly surveys the assembly. Most of them are recent converts to Christianity, many from Buddhist backgrounds. Some are non-Christians, spouses of members, or visitors invited by their friends.

The pastor speaks. "Now we come to the time when we bring our offerings to the Lord. With all respect, I should say to our visitors that this is not a collection of money. This is not a collection for charity. Those who are not Christians are not permitted to contribute to this offering.

"This is a privilege, a spiritual and holy ritual for those who believe in the Lord Jesus Christ and are baptized. This is their opportunity to respond to God's love and grace. It is their opportunity to fulfill their loving obligation as the children of God as they return part of the money they have received from God to build the church and reach out to the world. Again, those who are not Christians are not permitted to contribute to this offering." ("We Don't Want Your Money," *Lutheran Witness,* November 1992, 261. By the author.)

That's a new one! Or is it?

The Old Testament speaks often of offerings which are unacceptable to God—e.g., Genesis 4:5; Proverbs 15:8; Isaiah 1:11, 66:3; Jeremiah 6:20, 14:12; and Amos 5:22. In Acts 8:9–24, Peter told a man who was captive to sin, "May your money perish with you" (v. 20). And in 3 John 7, the apostle notes that he received "no help from the pagans."

These principles also relate to the Christian's reasons for giving, as the pastor in the Asian church noted. Paul wrote the Philippian Christians (4:17) that they should have an offering, but added in effect that they needed the spiritual exercise. Paul didn't need the money; rather, the people needed the opportunity to give. They needed the spiritual discipline of stewardship. God doesn't need our money either. We need God. And we need the opportunity to serve and worship him with our time, talent, and treasure.

So, only Christians can bring a true offering of praise and thanks to God. And when they do, it must be for the right reason.

Now, is that your understanding of what the Christian life, and stewardship of one's income and possessions, is all about? What did the pastor in the Asian congregation say? "This is a privilege, a spiritual and holy ritual for those who believe in the Lord Jesus Christ and are baptized. This is their opportunity to respond to God's love and grace. It is their opportunity to fulfill their loving obligation as the children of God as they return part of the money they have received from God to build the church and reach out to the world."

**The Rich Man**

How often do you and I instead become like the rich man in one of Jesus' parables? Before I recall it, let me stress that it is not wrong to be rich. Riches rightly earned are a great blessing from God. It is only the inordinate love of money that is wrong.

And that's the mistake of that one rich man in the parable. Remember it?

> There was once a rich man who had land which bore good crops. He began to think to himself, "I don't have a place to keep all my crops. What can I do? This is what I will do," he told himself; "I will tear my barns down and build bigger ones, where I will store the grain and all my other goods. Then I will say to myself, Lucky man! You have all the good things you need for many years. Take life easy, eat, drink, and enjoy yourself!" But God said to him, "You fool! This very night you will have to give up your life; then who will get all these things you have kept for yourself?" (Luke 12:16–20 TEV)

Whatever it is, whether it is the way we use the abilities God has given us or the way we spend our time—or paycheck or pension—when we are living for self first, we are not heeding the call of our God in our text, "You shall love the LORD your God with all your heart ..."

You and I need to repent, to turn, to change from our self-centeredness and hesitancy and to give our all to Christ. When Scripture says, "My son, give me your heart, And let your eyes observe my ways" (Prov. 23:26 NKJV), we are to respond lovingly, "With all my heart … I will obey your commands!" (Psalm 119:145 TEV).

This matter of handing over our whole self to Christ is at the very heart of our Christian faith. Paul writes, "For we know that our old self was crucified with [Christ] so that the body of sin might be done away with, that we should no longer be slaves to sin" (Rom. 6:6). "For you died, and your life is now hidden with Christ in God" (Col. 3:3). As Sheldon Turner said, "The Christ of the cross isn't going to become real to you until you come to terms with this hard core of reality at the heart of Christianity. How could he be real to you when you—not He—are still at the center of your life?" (Quoted in Catherine Marshall, *Beyond Ourselves* [Carmel, New York: Guideposts Associates, Inc., 1961], 188)

## The Mystery and the Paradox

Chad Walsh, an Anglican clergyman, put it this way in his classic book *Campus Gods on Trial* ([New York: Macmillan, 1962], 87):

> Here is the mystery and the paradox. The person who uses his freedom to give his "I" into the hands of God, there to be remade in the image of Christ, is really only lending it. For God gives it back. One day, when you least expect it, he returns it to you, much improved from the scrubbing and alterations it has received.

We may think we are surrendering to a master, but he is raising us as sons and daughters. It is only in going through this process—empowered totally by the Holy Spirit—that we can truly give Christ our all. As Luther said, "The recognition of sin is the beginning of salvation." (Source unknown) Charlie Brown often has said, "The theological implications of this are staggering." We are saved by grace through faith alone in Christ's death on the cross for us. Through faith alone. This is not an act we perform to be justified before God, but it is God at work in us.

Now we are called to follow him. But Christ is not just an example we are to follow. That is what we call "moralistic thinking." And it is a false understanding of the way the Gospel works.

Moralism holds up certain Christ-like qualities—dedication, self-denial, and the like—and then says, "Work on these traits and you'll be a good Christian." But the evil lies in not seeing that these ideals are *results of the Gospel*. They are not something we can do. We do not focus on "dedication" as a quality in Christ's character which we want to emulate, for we fail utterly; we can't do anything. Rather, we focus on his death on the cross for us. "For it is God who works in you to will and to act according to his good purpose" (Phil. 2:13).

Therefore, we look to Christ's commitment for and to us; and by the power of the Holy Spirit in us, we respond back with our commitment: Christ in me.

**Stewardship Sunday**

Note that on this Stewardship Sunday we have not been talking about money but about total dedication to Christ, empowered by the Holy Spirit. God wants all of you. He wants more than a wise stewardship of the material things he has entrusted to you. "My son, my daughter, give me your heart," he says, "your whole heart."

A certain mother frequently took trips abroad, sending her daughter lavish gifts from the various places she visited. On one of the daughter's birthdays, the mother sent a very beautiful, expensive vase. But the daughter, after tearing off the wrapping, tossed the gift aside, and cried, "Oh, Mother! I don't want any more gifts. No more flowers, no more vases, no more trinkets! Mother, I only want you! *You!" (Three Thousand Illustrations,* 170)

Similarly, God says, "I want *you* today."

As your pastor, I have not been giving you a laundry list of things to do with your pocketbook, but I have asked you to focus on your Savior. For when you love God with all your heart, a caring response to him of your time and service and material blessings will *spontaneously* flow back to him.

## Look to Jesus

Therefore, I call you to look to Jesus, "the author and finisher of *our* faith, who for the joy that was set before Him endured the cross, despising the shame, and has sat down at the right hand of the throne of God" (Heb. 12:2 NKJV).

Let us pray:

You asked for my hands
that you could use them for your purpose.
I gave them for a moment and then withdrew,
for the work was too hard.

You asked for a mouth to speak out
against injustice.
I gave you a whisper
that I might not be accused.

You asked for my eyes
to see the pain of poverty.
I closed them
for I did not want to know.

You asked for my life
that you might work through me.
I gave you a fractional part
that I might not get involved.

Lord, forgive me for calculated efforts
to serve you only when
it is convenient to do so—

Only in places where it is safe to do so.
Only with those who make it easy to do so.

Father, forgive me, renew me,
and send me out as a usable instrument
That I may take seriously
the meaning of your cross.

(Marileen Zdenek, in *Newsletter* of Shepherd of the Valley Lutheran Church,
Orinda, California, quoted in *For Example,* 69)

# Whatever Is Good

## Romans 2:14–15 and Titus 3:1–8

[The preacher has due respect for the church year and does not violate the liturgical calendar. The world's agenda does not dictate to the church and override its historic celebration of the mighty acts of God as they have been observed in the pericopes. At the same time we are not insensitive to the context in which our people live (Memorial Day, Labor Day, Mother's Day, Father's Day, etc). Therefore, resources are offered here that can be used in connection with some of these occasions. Appropriate reference to the propers for the day will of course be included by the preacher. Mervin A. Marquardt suggests the following outline for Memorial Day.]

*Introduction:* Memorial Day has become for many a day to remember both the war dead as well as family members who have died. I suggest we take the observance one step further and thank God for *all* who have sacrificed for our good— including in that "all" everyone, Christian or not.

   I.  Thank God for the sacrifices of those who have gone before.

      A.  God works through and for the good of whomever he wills.

         For example, he raised up Cyrus for the sake of Israel (Is. 44:28–45:7, especially v. 5b). See also God's reminder that he was behind the migrations of the Cushites, the Philistines, and the Arameans as well as those of the Israelites (Amos 9:7).

      B.  We have benefited from the good, even of unbelievers.

         Examples: The deists among the founding fathers; non-Christians who have given their lives for their country; avowed atheists who have advanced the benefits of science and medicine.

Romans 2:14-15: Unbelievers are capable of doing things of which consciences can approve (even if those good things are not good enough for salvation). The purpose of the Second Table of the Law, including the Law written in our hearts by nature, is the good of society—similar to God's reason for establishing government (Romans 13:1-4a).

II. We ask God to help us also to sacrifice for others, for our family and neighbors, for our country, for the world.

    A.  Our motivation: Jesus' sacrifice for us.

Titus 3:1-8: "Be subject ... be obedient ... be ready to do whatever is good ... toward all men. ... Stress these things, so that those who have trusted in God may be careful to devote themselves to doing what is good."

Note the progression: Faith, trust in God, comes *before* doing whatever is good toward all men. And once there is faith, there also are good works.

We who know and trust the Triune God for all we are, have, and will become—we have been freed from worrying about ourselves. We are, therefore, free to spend our energies for the sake of others.

    B.  Our goal: To serve society, doing good to all.

While we Christians want all to believe and to come to the knowledge of salvation, Jesus calls us to love even our enemies. He reminds us that he already loves them and blesses them with his sun and rain (Matt. 5:44-48).

Example: the servant girl who directed Naaman to a cure for his leprosy (2 Kings 5:1-3).

# The Art of Competing with Yourself

1 Corinthians 12:1-11

One time in the Peanuts cartoon series, one of the small fries asked Charlie Brown if he would like to have been Abraham Lincoln. He paused thoughtfully for a moment and said, "Well, now, I don't know. I'm having a hard enough time being just plain old Charlie Brown."

We all have difficulty living with ourselves—accepting ourselves as we are, with all our limitations and the responsibilities that come with whatever gifts we have. And we certainly have difficulty living with other people, different as they are from each of us. One study showed that Lutherans are more prone to accept people of a different color and creed than they are willing to accept those of a lifestyle or political affiliation different from their own. (Source unknown)

The difference of gifts—it's quite a problem, isn't it, accepting our differences and our radically different personalities in the home, in our congregation, in all our relationships in the world?

On Labor Day we honor the working person. But today I'd like to deal with a deeper issue than just your work in the world. I'd like to deal also with your work in the church, and more specifically, the particular gifts you have to work, gifts that the Holy Spirit has given each one of you.

Let's examine these issues today on the basis of our text and see (1) our dependence on the Holy Spirit for the Christian faith and life that we have; (2) the varieties of gifts, service, and working that God evidences among us; and finally (3) that it is one and the same Spirit, Lord, and God who moves among us according to his own will, giving to us, his children, all his bountiful blessings.

Our theme: <u>We can plan and execute our daily work totally apart from God, but he calls us to depend on the Spirit's power</u>

and guidance for what we do and to affirm our difference of gifts.

### *The* Spiritual Gift: the Holy Spirit

After one of the best-known atheists of our generation spoke on TV, a young man in the audience spoke of his conversion and accepting Christ as his Savior. The atheist looked over her shoulder at him disdainfully and shot back, "I want nothing to do with that man Jesus Christ! Young man, I'm ashamed of you! Why don't you learn to stand on your own two feet and accept responsibility for who and what you are and not pass the buck to someone else!" (From a TV program viewed by the author)

Apostasy and rejection of the man from Nazareth are hardly new in our day, not any more than when our Lord was on this earth. But denial of Christ takes place not only by open statements such as these. You and I can do so too by lives of practical atheism—planning our work, pursuing the hourly routine, without so much as giving God a thought or asking his guidance and blessing on what we are doing. As far as putting our lives and plans in his hands is concerned, we can say in effect, "Who cares?" But as Luther says, "We daily sin much and indeed deserve nothing but punishment."

That's why we need the forgiveness of sins. That is why Christ died. That is the Gospel: the forgiveness of sins. The Gospel is not, as some today say, freedom to do my own thing. The Gospel is God forgiving me through what happened on Calvary and in the now-empty tomb so that through the power of the Holy Spirit I can now say, "Jesus is Lord"—*my* Lord, *my* Savior, *my* Redeemer, the one I serve with the gifts he has given me.

### Varieties of Gifts

These being the central truths of our redemption—whose we are, who we are, and what it's all about—Paul moves quickly to the central point of today's text. He speaks of the different gifts we have as Christ's men and women and differences in the way we use them.

## God's Gifts to You

What is your gift? How do you conceive of yourself? Psychiatrists tell us that each person has three basic drives or needs: acceptance, affection, and achievement. Look at those again. Note that they're tied together with something else, not so much with what others think of you but primarily of what you think of yourself. Some words of Paul are apropos here: "Do not think of yourself more highly than you should. Instead, be modest in your thinking, and judge yourself according to the amount of faith that God has given you" (Rom. 12:3 TEV). This calls for a genuine humility, a quiet recognition of the capacities God has given you, balanced by your limitations. It means knowing your shortcomings but making a full and responsible use of your abilities to the glory of God.

In brief, accept the limits of personality potential with which God has endowed you. Stop competing with other people and with situations over which you have no control. Don't just ask yourself, "Am I successful?"—that is, in terms of the standards measured only by competitive supremacy. But ask how well you are carrying out the tasks God has given you, granting the limitations of your abilities. If you must compete, compete with yourself. Ask, "Does my record show faithfulness before God, giving him the glory?" Remember, "It is required in stewards that a man be found faithful" (1 Cor. 4:2 KJV). Not always successful or effective, but faithful. Knowing the gifts you have—and do not have—you can go on in faith towards a fuller service to our Lord in whatever position in life you may have.

## God's Gifts in Others

Do you accept God's gifts in other people, gifts he gave to them just as he has given you yours? Think of someone close to you in your family, school, or some other relationship. Peter

A. Bertocci's words that I will quote refer particularly to man and wife, but the principles apply across all our friendships with others. Bertocci says that the other person's worth is established by God; therefore, I am not to love this individual just because I "like" him or her. That relationship is enhanced by a certain vision that is not centered in either person but on God, for he is the third partner. Bertocci's words:

> I am to love her so that in and through this marriage she may find new depths and ranges to her being, in her response to all others, and to God. In the last analysis, I am not to be pleased, but she is to grow in the fullness of the nature God allowed her. ("What Makes a Christian?" *The Christian Century,* LXXVI 18 [May 1959])

And now catch these words of Bertocci: "I am to catch God's vision of her." Think of the dimensions of that statement! As you live and love and work together with other people in this parish, at home, in the business world, you are to "catch God's vision" of that person. What a challenge! What a different way of looking at each other! Anne Morrow Lindbergh had a phrase in *Gift from the Sea:* "Him that I love, I wish to be free even from me!" (New York: Pantheon Books, Inc., 1955)

This is our goal: Having accepted ourselves by the power of the Holy Spirit as forgiven sinners, we can now accept others. We free them, with their uniqueness and difference, and help them become the people God wants them to be, not what we wish they were nor what we would like to mold them into. Remember, God gave you that friend, that pastor, that child, that working associate, that boss, that life's partner. That person is God's present to you, with all her or his gifts—and with all the shortcomings.

A little girl in a wealthy family invited her classmates to her birthday party. Most of the children also came from a rather well-to-do background, except one 8-year-old in the group, who particularly liked the birthday girl. The 8-year-old had gone to considerable piggy-bank expense to select a present for her more affluent playmate. But when she presented it to her friend, the birthday girl took one look at it and, with a disdainful toss of her head, cast it aside and walked back to her other presents.

"But I picked it out *just for you!*" wailed the little girl, utterly crushed by the rejection. Then she followed the lass with the haughty air across the room and asked almost beseechingly, "Don't you like my present?" (*The Unlocked Door,* 33–34)

"Don't you like my present," God asks to you, "the presents of your body, your mind, your home, your spouse, your parents, all that you are and have? I have chosen these things *just for you.* Certainly, some of these circumstances you may change with my blessing. But 'I know the thoughts that I think toward you … thoughts of peace, and not of evil' [Jer. 29:11 KJV]. I know your needs far better than you do yourself. Don't you like my present?"

Therefore, I encourage you: As you look at the things and people and circumstances around you, look for the ways God has gifted them to be a blessing to you—and thank God for doing so.

## The Ways of Service

This leads us to other aspects of these different gifts: "There are different ways of serving, but the same Lord is served" (1 Cor. 12:5 TEV).

One activist churchwoman, as she saw a group of parents painting the church basement, said, "Now those are the active ones!" (Comment heard by the author)

Her comment may have been well intentioned. But others have made similar statements as a way of saying that those are the more *spiritual* members, those who attend every church-sponsored event. But while some parents were painting the basement, others may have been doing more for the kingdom of God by staying home and building a Christian family. Not every one has the same gift or role of service or work in the church.

On the other hand, the fellowship of the church is the place where people with all different kinds of backgrounds and lifestyles should be able to channel their God-given gifts. A young woman was once invited to meet others in the church by attending the Bible class, a congregational dinner, and so on—more than just the church service, which to date was the extent of her involvement in the congregation. To which she replied with a look of mock horror, "Oh, Pastor, don't ask me to get involved with people. I might get to know them better and find out they are just as hypocritical as I am." (Comment heard by the author)

What a tragic view of the church! It's in the church—with our different capacities for service, with our different personalities and lifestyles—that we learn how to work together, disparate though we are in our approaches to our problems and goals. It's in the church where the Holy Spirit provides the oil of his love to permit us to work together, smoothing out the rough edges of different sexes, ages, generations, and interests. Here it is that the one Spirit makes unity out of diversity and completeness out of all our imperfections.

## The Same Spirit, Lord and God

That's how Paul concludes our text. "It is one and the same Spirit who does all this; as he wishes, he gives a different gift to each person" (v. 11 TEV). This is the heart of our Christian faith, isn't it? The Spirit gives the power—the power by which we are converted to Christ, the power by which we daily exercise our gifts in God's kingdom.

Robert Ingersoll, the famous atheist of some decades ago, traveled widely across the country, lecturing to large groups of people. It is said that at one time he sought to show how the miracle of Lazarus being raised from the dead by Jesus was just a trick to bolster Jesus' waning fortunes. Lazarus was a good friend of Jesus, and he would pretend to have died, Ingersoll said, be dressed in grave clothes by his friends, and secretly be "buried." Then, as Jesus would pass by the sepulcher some days later, he would give the clue by calling Lazarus' name. Thereupon, Lazarus would come forth from the tomb, and everybody would think that Christ had performed a miracle and that he was really God. To clinch his point, Ingersoll said to the audience, "Can anyone tell me, now, why Jesus said, 'Lazarus, come forth'?"

An old Christian in the back got up and said, "Yes, I will tell you why my Lord said 'Lazarus, come forth.' Because if he had not said 'Lazarus,' he would have had the whole graveyard of Bethany coming out to him!" (*Three Thousand Illustrations,* 557–58)

Our Lord could have made a whole cemetery come to him, but neither you nor I come to God under our own power. "Ye have not chosen me, but I have chosen you" (John 15:16 KJV). In the blessed Sacrament of our Baptism, he called us and claimed us and made us his very own. By his Word, in the Scriptures and in the holy Eucharist, he feeds us daily. And as he wills, he gives us each a different gift or gifts—different personalities, different lifestyles, different areas for service and working in the church.

God made you. He wants you to be yourself, forgiven daily by the shed blood of Jesus Christ, empowered to do not your own thing but God's thing in your own way. And he gave you other people with different lives—and different gifts. Don't you just love his presents?

# The Woman of Noble Character

## Proverbs 31:28–31

[As noted in the introductory remarks to the Memorial Day sermon outline, the preacher will make appropriate reference to the propers for the day. The author assumes that whenever Mother's Day falls on Pentecost, that celebration of God and his work will supersede the secular observance.]

A true story: Alcohol had gotten the best of a certain woman and was the primary reason she became homeless, a bag lady who lived on the streets. To quote those who knew her, she was "a disgusting, drunken, foul-mouthed, mean old bum." Her body always smelled. You never would have invited her to your home.

One evening, just before Thanksgiving Day, a relative of hers got a call from the police. They wanted to know if the old lady was related to this particular family. The family was surprised to find out their long-lost aunt was still alive. Because she had never contacted the family, they presumed she had died long ago.

The family went downtown to get the homeless bag lady and invited her into their home to stay for Thanksgiving dinner the next day. Then they bathed her, cleaned her up, and gave her a nice dress to wear.

On Thanksgiving Day, as the prayer was being said, the old lady began to sob uncontrollably. Finally when she could talk, she explained that she was so very happy. She said if she had ever known that her family still loved her, she wouldn't have lived on the streets for the last 12 years. She is still with the family to this day. (*Windows into the Lectionary,* 62)

How different that experience is from the lives of most of us! How thankful many of us are for mothers and fathers whom we still may have with us and to whom we can personally show our love and affection!

But what another story it is when we fail to be God-fearing parents or when we do not show love and care for those who bore us and nurtured us through the years. And that brings me to my theme today: <u>Although we can become forgetful and uncaring, God calls some of us to be God-fearing parents, and he calls all of us to honor the gift of parents.</u>

The four verses of the text read earlier are from the well-known last chapter of the book of Proverbs. Verses 10 to 31 are described in the NIV as "Epilog: The Wife of Noble Character." The picture painted there of a pious, thrifty woman is so graphic, I would like to read it in its entirety. As I read, recall with thankfulness the times you have seen these qualities in a mother or grandmother who, as verse 30 says, truly "feared the Lord" (*fear*, meaning deep awe and reverence towards God). Ask yourself—whether mother, father, or single person—how well you measure up to the "noble character" Scripture here described.

[Read vv. 10–31.]

Today as we honor all mothers, those last four verses are particularly apropos.

[Re-read vv. 28–31.]

Are there times—whether you are a mother, father, or single—that the description "fears the Lord" has not been descriptive of your life? Or are there times when as a mother—or whatever your role—you have doubted God's care for you in the demanding responsibilities of your role?

Let me tell you a story about an elderly Christian lady who had a dream. Do you see yourself in one of the three women in the story?

In her dream, this woman saw three others at prayer, asking God to deliver them out of their troubles and suffering. As they were praying, Jesus drew near to them. As he approached the first of the three, he bent over her in tenderness and grace, with smiles full of radiant love, and spoke to her in accents of purest, sweetest music. Leaving her, he came to the next, but only placed his hand upon her bowed head and gave her one look of loving approval. The third woman he passed almost abruptly without stopping for a word or a glance.

The woman in her dream said to herself, "How greatly he must love the first one! To the second he gave his approval, but none of the special demonstrations of love he gave the first. And the third must have grieved him deeply, for he gave her no word at all, not even a passing look. I wonder what she has done and why he made so much difference between them."

As she tried to account for the action of her Lord, Jesus himself stood by her and said, "O woman, how wrongly you have interpreted me! The first kneeling woman needs all the weight of my tenderness and care to keep her feet in my narrow way. She needs my love, thought, and help every moment of the day. Without it she would fail and fall. The second has stronger faith and deeper love, and I can trust her to trust me however things may go and whatever people do.

"The third, whom I seemed not to notice and even to neglect has faith and love of the finest quality, and her I am training by quick and drastic processes for the highest and holiest service. She knows me so intimately and trusts me so utterly that she is independent of words or looks or any outward intimation of my approval. She is not dismayed or discouraged by any circumstances through which I arrange that she shall pass; she trusts me when sense and reason and every finer instinct of the natural heart would rebel, because she knows that I am working in her for eternity, and that what I do, though she knows not the explanation now, she will understand hereafter. I am silent in my love beyond the power of words to express. Also I am silent in my love for your sake that you may learn to love and trust."

What a great God you and I have! He is always there for you, even when he is seemingly silent. (Adapted from Charles E. Cowman, *Streams in the Desert*, [Vepery, Madras, India: Evangelistic Literature Service, 1982], 44–45)

We can see both judgment (Law) and mercy (Gospel) as

we apply this story to ourselves. There is judgment when, as a mother (or father or single person), we fail to trust God's presence in our trials. But there is comfort when we know that in our lonely or frenetic hours, Jesus is at our side.

The point: We are called to "fear, love, and trust in God above all things" (as Luther explains the First Commandment).

Second, do we always fulfill the words of our text, "Her children arise and call her blessed; her husband also, and he praises her" (v. 28); "Let her works bring her praise" (v. 31)? Today we *do* thank God for our mothers and fathers and grandparents. By God's grace we renew our own pledge to "fear the Lord" as the woman of noble character here does.

Note that fearing the *Lord* is the key emphasis here. He is the sole source of Christian character. Whether we are mother, father, or single, we don't work on doing "noble things" (v. 29) or fearing the Lord (v. 30). We don't work on traits of Christian virtue. For as sinners we fail utterly and "fall short of the glory of God" (Rom 3:23).

But Christ in us (Col. 1:27) does that which we are unable to do. Through his death on the cross for us and by his resurrection, we are forgiven and called to the fruits of faith, empowered totally by the Holy Spirit.

The Gospel is what *Christ* has done and is doing for us. The acts we perform, "noble things" and "being God-fearing," these are the *result* of the Gospel, the result of the Holy Spirit at work in our hearts. "It is God who works in you to will and to act according to his good purpose" (Phil. 2:13).

Therefore, on this Mother's Day, we ask God's forgiveness as mothers, fathers, or singles for where we have failed to be the "little Christs" he has called us to be. And we thank God for his power and grace working in us as parents, teachers—signposts and role models for others. And we thank God for our parents—with us now or already with the Lord in heaven.

A woman in a small discussion group had been listening to others talk about the happiest moments of their lives. Suddenly she interrupted them and said, "You know, I really don't think I belong to this group." And then she went on to describe her miserable childhood, her arguing parents, and the father who deserted the family.

The mother tried to make ends meet—they were destitute. But then one night, near Christmas, she said, "When we got home, we discovered that the front door was locked and all the shades drawn. My mother had the only key, but she had taught us to pry open a window on our long front porch so we could crawl in. So I opened the window and pushed the shade up so I could climb through into the living room.

"Then I just stared. There in the corner of that bare room was a scraggly Christmas tree with lights on it. And underneath, in the soft glow of those lights, were two doll bassinets with live-skin dollies in them. We couldn't imagine where our mother had gotten the money for such gifts."

She paused, remembering the scene, and then concluded, "And that was the happiest moment in my life." (Adapted from Keith Miller, *The Scent of Love*, 183)

What was the happiest moment of your life? Truthfully, although most of us were not aware of it at the time, it was when God brought us into his family through the Sacrament of Holy Baptism. But we also rejoice in other happy times in our families, especially today when we honor a loving mother—or father or grandparent—who gave us the gift of such "most happy moments." Yes, we thank God for those who first brought us to the baptismal font, taught us how to pray, brought us to church, nurtured us, and who "feared the Lord!" We "arise and call [them] blessed!"

# Father, Who's Following You?

Deuteronomy 6:5–9, 20–25

[A similar version of this sermon first appeared in *Concordia Pulpit Resources,* vol. 6, part 3 (June 2—September 8, 1996), 55–56.]

In Norway, the great ships cruise offshore from the southernmost tip of the nation to its northernmost coastlands. The ships are not only the pride of the country but also bind it together commercially. When a ship goes down, the entire nation watches in stunned silence.

A large vessel did go down in a fjord one night. But those listening to the radio were shocked to hear that a smaller vessel sank soon afterwards in exactly the same spot! Everyone wondered how such a strange coincidence could take place. Upon investigating it was learned that the smaller vessel had not been using its navigational gear. It simply followed the larger ship, thinking nothing could happen to it. (*For Example*, 84–85)

Father, who's been following you?

It's a grave responsibility to be a Christian father. Martin Luther noted this when he began his *Small Catechism* with the words, "As the head of the family should teach [the Christian truths] in a simple way to his household." Any instruction done by others—a pastor, Sunday school teacher, etc.—is done in the place of the parent, for God has given the primary responsibility to parents.

In our nation Father's Day is being observed today. But the biblical implications of being a Christian father apply also to mothers, grandparents, older brothers and sisters to whom little brothers and sisters look up, to all teachers, and to every single person in a leadership role. So, I ask the question of all of you here today: Who's following you?

My theme: <u>Although we often fail to live a Christian lifestyle, God equips us to exemplify faithfulness to Christ in all we say and do before others.</u>

Scripture has much to say about fathers and all of us who are being watched. Listen to what God's Word tells us in Deuteronomy 6:5, "Love the LORD your God with all your heart and with all your soul and with all your strength." Our lives are to be focused on God, not on ourselves. That's often our basic problem. We're looking in the wrong direction. Whatever your leadership situation in life, are you getting the proper focus?

Lord, direct me
not to focus my concern
on my stress
and anxiety
but rather
on you

Let me thankfully realize
that all in my daily walk
which is
good true lovely
heartwarming
joyous
exhilarating
comes
from you

Let my dreams
and aspirations
lead me upward
to you

that I may
be filled with
wonder admiration
awe
and worship
of you

Then the pressures
will be put
in proper perspective
the focus clear
the picture in
true proportion
you

(Prayers for People Under Pressure, 9. Used by permission)

## We return to Deuteronomy, verses 6 and 7:

These commandments that I give you today are to be upon your hearts. Impress them on your children. Talk about them when you sit at home and when you walk along the road, when you lie down and when you get up.

Talk about them *when?* All the time! Not just during an hour of so-called "quality time." Charles Swindoll vividly recalls the time he was caught in the undertow of too many commitments in too few days. He soon was snapping at his wife and children, gulping down his food at mealtimes, and feeling irritated at unexpected interruptions throughout the day. Soon things around his home started reflecting the pattern of his hurry-up style. It was becoming unbearable.

He recalls one evening after supper when his younger daughter, Colleen, spoke to him. She wanted to tell him something important that had happened to her at school that day. She hurriedly began, "Daddy-I-wanna-tell-you-somethin'-and-I'll-tell-you-really-fast."

Swindoll says he suddenly realized her frustration, and he answered, "Honey, you can tell me, and you don't have to tell me really fast. Say it slowly."

He says he will never forget her answer, "Then *listen* slowly." (Adapted from Charles Swindoll, *Stress Fractures* [Portland: Multnomah, 1990])

Verse 8 of Deuteronomy 6, stressing our need to follow the commandments of the Lord, says, "Tie them as symbols on your hands and bind them on your foreheads. Write them on the doorframes of your houses and on your gates."

The point is that we humans need visual reminders of who and what we are. Which Christian symbols do you have in your home? A cross? A picture of Christ? Other Christian art? Maybe even a prayer niche, with a votive shelf and a kneeler?

A seminary student told about his 4-year-old boy who walked into a friend's home and said, "Oh, Daddy, this is a church house, just like ours!" Is yours a "church house"? (Comment heard by the author)

A foreign student had been in the home of a Christian girl-friend over the Christmas vacation. Before leaving for school, the girl's mother asked the international student if she had enjoyed her stay with them. To this the young girl, not a Christian, replied, "Yes, I enjoyed my stay very much. But one thing puzzles me. Do you not have a God-shelf in your home? In my country everybody has a God-shelf in their house. Do you worship your God only in church?"

That was an incisive question. So many Christians still have very few things in their homes that symbolize the Christian life and the center of our Christian faith, our Lord and Savior. (*For Example*, 216)

Deuteronomy 6:20–25 adds that this training of our children is ongoing.

> In the future, when your son asks you, "What is the meaning of the stipulations, decrees and laws the LORD our God has commanded you?" tell him: "We were slaves of Pharaoh in Egypt, but the LORD brought us out of Egypt with a mighty hand. Before our eyes the LORD sent miraculous signs and wonders—great and terrible— upon Egypt and Pharaoh and his whole household. But he brought us out from there to bring us in and give us the land that he promised on oath to our forefathers. The LORD commanded us to obey all these decrees and to fear the LORD our God, so that we might always prosper and be kept alive, as is the case today. And if we are careful to obey all this law before the LORD our God, as he has commanded us, that will be our righteousness."

The Old Testament father was to remind his children repeatedly of the mighty acts of God. And so are we, as we recount his blessings to us today.

So the scriptural injunctions are clear. They are repeated in Proverbs 22:6: "Train a child in the way he should go, and when he is old he will not turn from it." And in Ephesians 6:4: "Fathers, do not exasperate your children; instead, bring them up in the training and instruction of the Lord."

Heavy stuff, being a Christian father! We need to be reminded again and again of the grave responsibility we have. There was a sixth-grade girl who brought home an assignment asking her to make detailed comments on two chapters of Scripture. It took her father two hours. Of course, he was only "helping" her. But it vividly reminded him again that he was ultimately responsible for her Christian training.

A boy ran away from home and headed for a large city. He left a note saying he had appreciated the presents his parents had given him over the years, but he couldn't cope with all the things he felt. What he'd really wanted was for them to listen to him. But they were always too busy. He concluded, "If anybody asks you where I am, tell them I've gone looking for somebody with time, because I've got a lot of things I want to talk about." (Robert A. Raines, *Creative Brooding* [New York: Macmillian, date unknown], 82)

Recall how our text stated (v. 5): "Love the LORD your God with all your heart." Serving God with all your heart includes being a parent with all your heart. It means bringing your child up as a Christian. It means keeping the promise made at your child's Baptism that he or she would be brought up in the true knowledge and worship of God, be taught the Ten Commandments, the Creed, the Lord's Prayer. It means that you place in your child's hands the Holy Scriptures, and bring him or her to church. And in all this you will point your child to Jesus, who by his death on the cross for our sins gives us eternal life.

Do you raise your child as if nothing else is more important than that child's spiritual future? You and I often fail in our obligations as fathers, as parents, as grandparents, as older brothers and sisters, as people in positions of leadership and authority. For that we need to repent, to turn, to change.

The Good News is that God does empower you to be the loving parent he has called you to be.

He himself is *the* Father. Recall Luther's explanation of the First Article:

> I believe in God, the Father Almighty, Maker of heaven and earth.
>
> *What does this mean?* I believe that God has made me and all creatures; that he has given me my body and soul, eyes, ears, and all my members, my reason and all my senses, and still takes care of them.
>
> He also gives me clothing and shoes, food and drink, house and home, wife and children, land, animals, and all I have. He richly and daily provides me with all that I need to support this body and life.
>
> He defends me against all danger and guards and protects me from all evil.
>
> All this he does only out of fatherly, divine goodness and mercy, without any merit or worthiness in me. For all this it is my duty to thank and praise, to serve and obey him.
>
> This is most certainly true.

All this our heavenly Father has done for us. Better, he gave his own Son into death on the cross. There Christ paid for all of our failures as examples of the Christian life to those who follow after us.

In this Pentecost season, as we see the blessed work of God the Father, Son, and Holy Spirit in our own day-to-day lives as Christians, may we, by God's grace, fulfill our high calling as parents and leaders of others.

Like this father:

> A man had a day off and decided to spend the time in a bawdy part of town. And so he slipped quietly away from his home and started across a snow-covered field toward his destination. He had not gone far before he heard a voice behind him.

It was his 6-year-old son, who said, "Go ahead, Daddy, I'm walking in your steps."

Shocked, the man stopped in his tracks. Then he picked up his son in his arms and, collecting his thoughts, said, "Now, What shall we do together today?" (Source unknown)

## What will you do together today?
## May it be a joyous, blessed day together!